skinny dipping

for margaret and fletcher collins
who pushed me into the water

and for katie lyle and sarah o'connor
who helped me stay afloat

contents

acknowledgments

Convention stipulates that both spouse and editor be acknowledged for putting up with all manner of writerly moods and eccentricities. I am, of course, grateful to my husband, the Chief, and my editor, Peter Burford, for their help and patience. The Chief also merits recognition for demonstrating with splashy, spouting exuberance that the urge to skinny-dip and the sport itself are never outgrown.

Then there are the others to whom convention does not mandate a nod but who nonetheless made significant contributions to the stories:

- Mariclaire Hale, who put the bathtub on the limestone ledge
- John Herington, who knows about Celsus, the River Styx, and other things not mentioned in the *Britannica*
- Laura Killingsworth, who knows her nursery rhymes
- Rodney Russ, who invited me to the Southern Ocean and realms not yet dominated by human time
- Curtis Seltzer, who has his own tales of how the water comes down at the gorge
- Nancy Sorrells, who has rounded up history's horned red cattle
- Larry Syzdek, who practices the quite real science of bubble-ology

To all of you and all the others who gave me water wings, my buoyant, heartfelt thanks.

skinny dipping

introduction

My swim in the birdbath qual-
ifies as skinny dipping, it certainly does. But I didn't recognize this aspect
of the swim until many years later, when it was brought to my adult attention by Epimetheus, the guardian spirit of afterthoughts and back-
ward glances. In his dilatory way, he also clarified a second aspect of the
episode, but I'll get to that in a moment. It's a good idea to keep things in

order, one-two-three, and the birdbath definitely came first. Without that full-to-brimming-over birdbath, there would have been no reason for peeling down to the buff and plunging in. But I wouldn't have called it skinny dipping back then. At the age of four, I probably didn't know the term.

Imagine these circumstances: a still and breathless summer afternoon, its blue sky innocent of clouds, and a silence broken only by cicadas and the milk cows lowing in the back pasture of my father's farm. Our big old house, its shingles painted forest green, sits amid a vast lawn, bounded by a flower border and a tall hedge. And over there at the edge of my mother's formal rose garden, a large birdbath atop a stout pedestal has been placed strategically near a clump of shrubs that offers instant cover to any birds startled at their ablutions. Add heat to this scene—not just any summer heat but heat of the sultry sort that makes old dogs lie panting in the shade and plops grown-ups into the well-cushioned wicker chairs on the porch. There they sip gin and tonic from sweating glasses and discuss matters of no interest whatsoever to a four-year-old.

That may not be where my parents and their friends, visiting from Detroit, had sequestered themselves on that torrid, blue afternoon, but it's a reasonable guess. It's also reasonable to suppose that wherever they were, whatever they were up to, water thoughts had not entered their heads—thoughts like filling the wading pool or turning on the sprinkler for a child to run through.

But I can offer facts along with these suppositions. One is that I could not see the grown-ups. More important, because I couldn't see them, it followed that they could not possibly see me. Nor was I alone. The friends had brought along Scotty, their towheaded four-year-old son.

Of course, we headed for the birdbath. It was, after all, the only accessible water in sight. Of course, we took off all our clothes. Four is quite old enough to know that you don't go swimming in your street clothes. You're supposed to wear a bathing suit, but if you don't have one handy, plain skin, thank you, will do very well. Of course, we climbed into the birdbath. Two children at once—that's how I know the birdbath was large. Out there under the summer sun, the water in that shallow, cast-concrete basin must have been warm if not downright hot, but oh it was wonderful. Scotty and I dipped our bare skins in that thrilling water. We splashed and giggled and squealed.

Of course, the noise attracted the grown-ups. In no way had being out of sight exempted us from parental vigilance. Epimetheus helped me figure that one out almost right away. But it took years before I understood the disapproval on their faces, in their voices, and the lack of gentleness with which they yanked us from the birdbath, covered us, and sent us to languish in separate corners. I'm sure that Scotty didn't understand this response any more than I did. Astonishing! Those grown-ups were behaving as if we'd done something bad, something not just bad but awful.

I would have been willing to admit to naughtiness and suffer some minor punishment. My parents had delivered many stern injunctions about never ever going in the water unless an adult was present. We'd been naughty, yes. But bad? Absolutely not. At that time in my life, even if the adults had tried to explain their objections to the coed nature of our skinny-dip, they'd have succeeded only in creating more bewilderment. Modesty, immodesty, exposure of private parts—these concepts had no meaning. Sometimes my two-year-old brother was diapered, sometimes not, and his penis was as much a given as other natural appendages—a milk cow's udder or the tail of a dog.

And, surprise, it turns out that those scowling adults ought to be thanked. I understand that too, now that I'm older than they were back then. The birdbath incident could have slipped into the limbo of things only vaguely remembered or not remembered at all. But because the grown-ups overreacted, because of their stern but most mysterious disapprobation, they gave me a memory—not only gave it, but guaranteed it. The colors and heat of that day are with me still, and the soft, cool, feathery, quite delicious sensations of water slipping over bare skin.

The dour and suspicious grown-ups of America have had their way for much too long. Skinny dipping—say those words out loud, especially in mixed, middle-class company, and faces undergo an immediate, peculiar transformation. Eyebrows lift, mouths twitch and purse, eyes narrow and assume a knowing, guilty glint. It's almost as if those present had been caught at something rude, crude, lewd, vulgar, and socially unacceptable, like flashing or picking their noses. Everybody's well acquainted with the term, and the acquaintance is hardly theoretical. But, though nobody pulls an emperor act and tries to pretend it isn't so, nobody says much either, just "Hmm" or "Yeah." Skinny dipping can be done only in the buff. Speaking about it seems tantamount, therefore, to taking off every last stitch of psychic clothing and standing there starkly exposed to the frowns and prurient snickers of the world. So the details of experience are kept under wraps.

Such a self-conscious response is only a matter of social convention like handshakes and smiles. But handshakes and smiles are disarming gestures meant to demonstrate good intentions towards strangers. False modesty does nothing of the sort. Culture and fashion have shaped that response, not instinct, and it's about as useful, as natural as a plastic flamingo or a grocery-store tomato.

Truth is, most of us contain a splashing, giggling, squealing child who knows without thinking that bare skin and water go together as wings go with air, roots with earth, and the phoenix with incendiary sun. And innocence belongs to us as it did to ancient Greek athletes, who never wore clothes for their footraces or boxing matches but rather oiled themselves till their nude bodies glistened in the sunlight. Innocence belongs to us as truly as to Japanese men and women in a communal bath. It belongs to us as blithely and freely as to the boys in George Bellows' 1907 painting *Forty-two Kids*.

Look at them—a whole passel of lanky, newly adolescent young'uns milling around and strutting their stuff at the old swimming hole. No matter that this swimming hole is located somewhere along the not-too-clean East River waterfront of New York City. On a hot summer's day, any water issues an invitation to jump in, and who are these kids to resist its seductions? Most of them already wear nothing but bare asses, and the few who haven't yet achieved that unencumbered state are peeling off shorts and shirts as fast as they can. Some stand or lie on an old, half-rotten dock with missing boards. Some sit, their toes dangling down toward the cool, wet darkness. One boy hangs over the water butt down, his heels hooked on the dock's edge, his arms held by another kid who looks as if he's about to let go—kersplash! Another boy bends down in the shallows to scoop up water and slosh it over his body. Farther out, others stand belly-deep in the stream splashing their buddies. And one buck-naked kid is neither here nor there, not on the old dock nor in the water, but spraddled in the air, all bony knees and cupcake rump, like an angel en route to a bellyflop. Oh yes!

In this lively painting, Bellows does not depict what a certain sort of prissiness calls "frontal nudity." But that's not the point. The painting does not mean to illustrate anatomy. Instead, it gives delighted thanks for the existence of swimming holes and summertime. Even more, it celebrates the conjoined innocence and sensuosity of an age-old rite that, for its fleeting moment, creates a perfect union of flesh and water.

I talk about skinny dipping a lot, of course. And once people understand that I'm not pressing for details, that my interest centers on the sport itself rather than on the circumstances of particular games, almost everyone agrees that skinny dipping is the most completely sensuous experience available to humankind. Shallow or deep, clear or tannin-stained, fresh or salty, tamed in a backyard pool or wild as a mountain stream, vast as an ocean, the water flows 'round and seeks us. It sparkles and swirls, surges and lapses. It splashes, rushes over rocks, whispers, breaks, and bubbles. It fills noses and mouths with a bromine reek, a coolness of trout and algae-covered stones, a tidal potpourri of seaweed, fish, and salt. And when it touches us, it drenches our bodies, every pore, every nerve, every last cell, with the purest pleasure. To skinny-dip is to drown in bliss.

Skinny dipping . . . Water would seem to be the basic requirement, a body of water surrounding, embracing an unclad human body. Rivers, lakes, curling breakers at the beach, backyard swimming pools—these are the likely venues for finding bliss. Others less obvious are not to be overlooked, such as garden sprinklers and pouring-down rain. In a pinch, even a birdbath will do. Or better, a bathtub, especially if it's like the one a friend installed once upon a time in the yard of her cabin on Irish Creek.

Out of a spring high on a steep, wooded, west-facing slope of the Blue Ridge, the long silver thread of Irish Creek spills down and down until it reaches the tucked-away clearing where the cabin stands. There the terrain becomes gentler, the creek less impetuous in its seaward rush. As it flows with a soft and glittering din along the edge of the yard, it's hardly more than ankle-deep—except for one stretch all of four yards long. In that place, the water comes up to the knees. That's the stretch to which those of us using the cabin repaired for summertime bathing of both the cooling-off kind and the soap-in-hand scrub-down kind. That is, till the bathtub arrived.

Oh what a tub! What an ample and sturdy Victorian tub! Made of porcelainized cast iron with claw and ball feet, it was found at a salvage dealer's, brought up the mountain on a heavy-duty pickup truck, and set—with monumental effort and cussing—on a flat, sunny limestone ledge behind the cabin. And on that plinth, in the complacently imperious manner of the jar that Wallace Stevens placed in Tennessee, the tub tamed the wilderness and took dominion everywhere. There was no plumbing, of course—no taps, no drainpipe. Anyone wanting to take a bath drew water at a hand pump and toted it tubwards two buckets at a time. Cool in the morning, if not downright icy, the water would warm to almost womblike coziness by midafternoon. But I never once used it for soaping down, no. The only proper way to handle that tub of sun-dazzled water was to strip down, climb in, and bask, toasting all of creation with a glass or two of wine. That qualifies, I'm sure, as skinny dipping of the finest sort, albeit in a man-made pond. Then, ten years ago, the tub was left behind, too ponderous to take back down the mountain, when my friend's lease on the cabin ran out. But for all I know, it still stands on its four claws and balls in the sun-bright clearing beside Irish Creek.

Is a body of water really needed, though, for a truly satisfying skinny dip? Is it the one absolutely necessary prerequisite, without which all else fails? It seems to me that, in sultriest July, sweat and the vagrant touch of a cooling breeze can certainly provide a pleasingly sensuous approxima-tion of the real thing. And wind all by itself, from light airs to full gale, provides endless opportunities for total immersion. So do the cavernous reaches of darkness.

But I know from long indulgence that some of the best and barest splashing comes without any water at all. Without any water, that is, ex-cept the stuff that seeps up quietly in memory or makes a flinging, springing rush through imagination. Nor is it necessary to take off one stitch of clothing. The only things that need to be shed are the habits that sometimes keep attention gliding straight down an easy, familiar route rather than letting curiosity make side excursions into the back-waters, streamlets, and swamps on either hand.

In these stories I jump into various waters of the kind validated by both science and everyday experience. Some are nearby—wild moun-tain rivers in Virginia and West Virginia, a salty estuary and a brackish creek in coastal North Carolina. Others are far away in distance or in time—the Mediterranean Sea of the first century A.D.; the cresting, laps-ing, eternally stormy and lonesome expanses of the Southern Ocean. I also follow imagination as it cannonballs, whooping and shouting, into the swimming holes and antic streams of good Mother Goose and the Brothers Grimm, and I grab hold of passing fancy, letting it take me wherever it's impelled on the deep, swift currents of myth and literature.

Sometimes my husband, the Chief, comes along—or stirs up the action in the first place. He's a retired chief petty officer with saltwater in his veins and a blue, piratical gleam in his eyes. And sometimes Sally, our dog, provides companionship on the adventures. Though I've heard of one or two others, she's the only Doberman I've ever met that regards water as a friendly element and goes for regular dips to cool off or retrieve the carcasses of just-cleaned fish. She's always dressed for the occasion and comes along most agreeably no matter where we go.

In company or alone, I often have no particular destination in mind but simply ride whatever wave or whirlpool sweeps me up. After all, where else but in rivering, hitherandthithering imagination do the waters of Babylon still rise, or the primal seas of Genesis? Where else the River Styx, the reflecting pool in which Narcissus adored his image, and the salty spate of tears wept by Niobe, who boasted that she was more fortunate and fecund than the gods and, for such presumption, such overweening pride, saw every one of her fourteen children destroyed? Where else might a rose bud and sprout at the bottom of the sea, or a chimney sweep develop gills?

Come with me. Take off the old habits. Plunge in.

skinny dipping

Non on recte recipit haec nos rerum natura nisi nudos. "This element—water—does not properly receive us unless we are naked."

So says Pliny, the Roman natural historian, though he'd not see those words as an enthusiast's recommendation for traipsing birthday-suited into the sea. He intends them, rather, as a plain man's censure of conspicuous consumption—the epicures devouring seafood brought in by the boatload and prepared in a thousand sumptuous ways, the fashionable and frivolous women who sally forth dripping from stem to stern with untold oysterbeds of pearls, the men who strut their vanity in woollen robes made crimson or purple with dye extracted drop by tiny drop from countless murex snails. With disgust and not a little anguish, he asked why his Roman compatriots find the acme of satisfaction in luxuries obtained only at horrific costs in human life. What possible link exists between the sea and our accoutrements? Water and waves did not create these goods to adorn our backs. It is enough, he cries, that we feed off the perils of fishermen without also using their dangers for personal bedizenment.

Pliny has a point, to be sure, but he entices me to look down a long corridor of time and watch him as he reclines on a bright Mediterranean shore. The season is summer—early August; the year, A.D. 79 or, as Pliny might think of it, the first year in the reign of the emperor Titus; the place, a Neapolitan seaside resort not far from Pompeii and Mt. Vesuvius. Pliny is prefect—admiral—of the fleet based at nearby Cape Misenum, one of Rome's major naval stations since the time of Augustus. Despite his rank, he's dressed in simple, undyed linen.

He's not alone but accompanied by an educated slave, who reads aloud from a book written on a roll of papyrus. Occasionally, the slave puts down the roll to copy on tablets the passages that have caught his ever-studious owner's attention. Today's language is Greek, and the passage just read is Aristotle's report that some animals change the color of their coats with a change in their drinking water. Aristotle says that rivers can influence coloration; sheep drinking from one river bear black offspring, while the same kind of sheep slaking thirst at a river just around the bend produce white lambs. Long before Mendel and Darwin, Pliny speculates about the causes of variability among different populations of the same species. "Make a note," he tells the slave. "Question: Might the color of otherwise identical sea animals be affected by differences in water between one bay and the next?"

The water that stretches before him looks molten with heat and silvery sunlight. At his house in Rome, after a modest lunch, he likes to lie outside and let the summer sun massage him while the eternal book is being read and excerpted. But this undulant water whispers, sizzles, swooshes, discouraging quietude. Pliny rises restlessly and strides down the beach to see what he can see. Who knows what might be stranded on this shore or what might surface in the waves? Still reading, not missing a beat, the slave follows.

Pearls of sweat bead Pliny's forehead. The day is ideal for a dip, but he frowns at the water not willing to wet even his toes. The sea frightens him as much as it fascinates. As admiral, he has seen his ships wrecked, his sailors drowned. As natural historian, he is all too aware of what lurks in the deeps. Not only does the sea's huge, glittering expanse of water shudder most lavishly, most excessively toward the horizon, but it produces so many nutrients on its own and gulps in so many more from the air above that it spawns an inordinate number of offspring.

The sea holds wonders—the sea cucumber that looks and smells like its vegetable counterpart; a tiny bivalve from which a miniature horse's head projects; a sea turtle living in the Indian Ocean that is so large that people on the coast can use its shell as a boat or as roofing for a whole house. The sea contains divinity made visible—frolicking Nereids and the Tritons that balance on fishtails and use their horse-forelegs to clutch trumpet shells on which they blow tunes that moan like the wind spilling out of a full sail. And the sea shelters monsters, such as foul-smelling cuttlefish that coil their arms around divers and shipwrecked sailors, fasten suction cups on the struggling men, and rip them apart. Pliny has not seen a cuttlefish in the waters off Naples, but the only chances he likes to take are those of the intellect, not the body. He has, however, risked several encounters with jellyfish. Though they do not pulse on the surface today, his flesh still remembers the burning itch of their stings. And he's absolutely leery of stingrays, which he has seen caught in the nets of fishermen, for it's said that their venomous five-inch barbs can penetrate armor like a spear and kill trees if driven into the roots.

He'd half-like, however, to come across the body of a Nereid on the beach, for it's been reported that these sea nymphs are covered entirely with bristling hair, even in those places where their forms are human. (He once examined seals during his military service in Gaul, but he makes no connection between that firsthand evidence and the second- or thirdhand reports.) But today, though the beach is littered with shells and with laughing, squealing holiday-makers, no Nereid washes up for his inspection.

No matter. Another nymph presents herself to his omnipresent, middle-aged curiosity. Petite, brunette, and seal-eyed, she's covered entirely with a smooth tan, at least in the places available to his gaze, nor does he need to imagine much. Wearing a scanty, two-piece outfit, she's tossing a beach ball bright as a rainbow and flirting with all the young men, some clad and some quite nude, who are at play within her giddy orbit. Her eye meets his but looks quickly away, rejecting his scholar's squint, wrinkles, thinning hair, and fuddy-duddy demeanor. But he didn't really leave the comforts of home to investigate the comparative anatomy of nymphs divine and mortal. The idea of water, if not its vast, imagination-taunting reality, has brought him here. The slave reads on.

And the sea surges softly toward Pliny's bare, sandy toes. He's tempted. Children are out there splashing in the water, not afraid of possible monsters nor of real mothers and nursemaids shouting at them to be careful. Two older bathers dash toward the briny, and one of them, a dumpling woman, bumps Pliny's arm in her rush. She's a-clatter with pearls, and her companion wears a bathing costume with a wide purple stripe. How sorely these two affront the sea's dignity.

Pliny does as he must. It may be that he also has a premonition that today is his last chance for a swim. In two weeks, on August 24, Vesuvius will blow. His quenchless curiosity will prompt him to view the eruption from a ship and then to go ashore to a friend's house on the south shore of the Bay of Naples. The house will be battered by hurtling rocks and shaken by tremors as the volcano cracks apart. Pliny will go outside where, ever the inquisitive observer, he will lie down on an old linen cloth. It is not stones nor ash but the inhalation of noxious vapors that will kill him.

Today, a sea breeze wipes Pliny's brow as he strips to the buff, dropping fears on the sand along with sweat-drenched clothes. The slave puts down the book. And Pliny wades in, chin up, arms outstretched to his sides. Water gives this naked man the silkiest of hugs. Soon, he's splashing as happily as any child.

Bare skin is the one and only right criterion for receiving water's gracious acceptance or any acceptance whatsoever from that element. But Pliny also seems to say something more: Stripping off not caution but the stale, crusty garments of preconception, peeling sensibility down to raw, new nakedness, is the only way to enter and be properly embraced by the world.

*   *   *

The last jar of tomatoes has just been pulled from the steaming canner. "C'mon," the Chief says, taking my hand. He leads me eagerly to the waterfront.

The water looks like consommé, golden brown and utterly transparent. Jellyfish have not seasoned this broth for the last week. Today, schools of fry and fingerlings—spot, croaker, anonymous others—dart near the bulkhead and cast quick shadows on the rippled sand below. Sun applies a mirror finish to the surface farther out; no breeze, no jumping fish, no boats mar the shine. The distant shore trembles, distorted by reflected light. Brow-mopping heat and the stillness of early afternoon may presage thunderstorms before supper. But right now the sky shows not a wisp of cloud. Right now the river rings its soundless bell. "Time to get exhilarated," as the Chief puts it. Time for skinny dipping.

Grinning, we shed our clothes and grown-up lives. The water tickles bare groins and bellies. How cool the river feels! Children again, giggling with residual naughtiness but not caring if anyone sees or hears, we launch our bodies forward, blending sweat with brine. The water covers heat-stung nakedness as comfortably as scales and coaxes our arms and legs into an almost forgotten response. We're speckled seatrout leaping and plunging, flounder hugging the bottom, bluefish putting on speed, whales spouting water. No, we're dolphins drunk on the music of laughter, and we're Proteus changing our shapes at will as the water keeps asking its ceaseless question, *Why did you leave me, why take to land?* The sea god advances, spear at the ready; the nymph is willing. Later, another transformation: We're turtles paddling lazily along with pale flippers, huge sea turtles with waterweeds of hair streaming from our bodies. We're a hundred years old, no, older than the idea of years. Our boneless shadows skate over the sunlit sand below. It is as if we have begun to dissolve, to return to an element once our only home.

But blood, warmer than water, rejects the sea. Shivering, we creep back to land, into the hot air that holds us burning between the natal ocean and our own dust. The Chief towels me dry and hugs me. From what unimaginable depths have we risen, from what abyss of myth and history and longing? On his skin I taste the salt.

touching

earth

Well! A small tank lumbers through the short grass at garden's edge. Camouflaged in grey-green armor plating splotched at random with charcoal black, it moves at a slow but deliberate pace that indicates both purpose and destination. Where is it going? And why?

I won't find out, but the answers aren't really important. Just watching this tiny, high-domed juggernaut is enough. And what better excuse to stop weeding the vegetable patch, at least for a little while? It's not every day that an Eastern Hercules beetle comes rolling by.

The pause is welcome. Though the calendar swears that the year has unrolled no farther than mid-May, the sun blazes down with the zest of July, and the bright blue North Carolina morning drips heat. I wear a bandanna tied around my brow, but still the sweat rolls down my forehead and falls off the end of my nose in large, juicy drops. The garden that was sown in April—root vegetables on the waning moon, light-loving crops as it grew full—begins to look like a jungle. Not one of the tender food plants can match the bursting, opportunistic energy, the sneaking tendrils or skyward thrusts, of Bermuda grass and Johnson grass, ragweed, pigweed, bindweed, goosefoot and dock, dog fennel and rabbit tobacco. The spaces between the rows have been tilled clean, but handwork is required to extract the competition that's elbowing out our hopes for a decent harvest. Despite the steamy weather, despite my natural-born laziness, I am offered no choice between staying cool and dry or getting hot and dirty, not if we are to savor homegrown vegetables this year. So here I am, swimming in sweat, glasses slipping down my nose as if it were a water slide, and fingernails packed with enough sandy loam to start another garden. And there's still one more fifty-foot row of beans to weed before lunch. Even so, it seems permissible to take a short break to watch a colossal Hercules beetle haul its two-inch dome through the grass.

Marching onward with unfaltering and measured tread, it is surely embarked on some labor as arduous as any performed by its ancient namesake, the hero Herakles. Let evil perish! Long live the good! The sight of the beetle conjures the myth. Herakles was set twelve punishing tasks that called for superhuman strength and sent him amid the earth's most perilous ugliness and its most astonishing beauty. He slew the man-killing Nemean lion and the venomous, many-headed Hydra. Without harming either, he captured first a sacred deer with bronze hooves and golden antlers and then a boar of extraordinary size and savagery. He cleansed a king's dung-filled stables by diverting two rivers to flow through them and carry away the filth. Then, slaughtering some, banishing the rest, he rid the land of a huge flock of predatory birds that used their brass feathers like arrows to shoot people down. Some of the other labors demanded that he steal horses, rustle cattle, and fetch golden apples from their orchard in the far Hesperides where the giant Atlas held the world upon his shoulders. And on his way to the dragon-guarded tree on which the apples grew, Herakles encountered another giant, Antaios, and killed him.

This monster was the son of Earth and Poseidon, lord of the oceans. One meaning of the name Antaios is "hateful," and hateful he was. To honor his father, Antaios constructed a temple of human skulls. When brave men attempted to stop his murderous work, their heads were simply added to the pile of building materials.

Enter Herakles. But even such a potent hero found it difficult to battle an enemy whose physical might seemed never to fail, no matter how grievous his wounds. Finally Herakles guessed the source of the giant's strength, that it rose anew each time he touched his mother, Earth. And Herakles killed Antaios by holding him high above the ground till all his power bled away into the empty air.

Trudging steadily on, the beetle enters the garden and disappears amid the overgrown bell peppers. Returning to my own labors—out, Johnson grass! out, out, ragweed and thistle!—I contemplate the peculiar story. It seems not only inappropriate but downright perverse for Earth to nurture such an evil being, to repeatedly restore his vigor and his very life. Granted that he was her son, but even mother love might balk at saving such as him. Out, Jimson weed—out with your roots, stem, blossoms, and prickers! I'll grub you up, remove you from your source of strength. Out—

Wait a minute. Earth is nurturing these brash green weeds, every last one of them. Supporting the useless along with the useful, the fatal monsters along with golden-antlered deer, Earth doesn't play favorites. The only ones who make such distinctions, the only ones capable of doing so, are human beings. And what are we but Herakles and Antaios, both of them and all at once, all tangled together?

Out, Bermuda grass, keep your tendrils in the lawn where they belong. Out, pigweed and ragweed. This is my day, not yours, for touching Earth, for finding not only present strength but its assurance in days to come. Maytime labor will bring a June harvest. We'll store Earth, as well: onions and garlic with braided leaves, green beans, carrots, corn on the cob, cucumbers and the dill with which to pickle them, butternut squash for eating plain or making pies, and always tomatoes that, fresh or preserved, retain the rich red heat of summer sun. Later, even in winter's most frigid darkness, that heat will rise fragrant and delicious. And we'll touch Earth again.

invitation

to a rainy day

It's raining.

Raining? No, the word "rain" is far too neutral, too paltry for what is drenching the North Carolina coast at Great Neck Point. The sky fitted the earth like a snug, grey, felted cap this morning when I waded out in the wide and salty river to fish the gill net. Before I'd hauled the catch ashore, the sprinkles had started, pocking the dark water like scattershot.

While I cleaned croaker and spot, the drops grew heavier, the far shore disappeared in fog. Now that packaged fish are in the freezer and I've exchanged my scale-covered fishing clothes for dry and ordinary garb, sozzle and showers and pure inundation have taken possession of the day. Mostly, the drops rat-a-tat on the trailer's roof like seeds pouring out of a hopper, but sometimes the quick, distinct sounds merge into one when the rain intensifies and the water falls in steady sheets. Rain rolls down the window, letting us see light but little else.

While Sally Doberman naps on the sofa, my husband, the Chief, inspects our old, weather-beaten trailer for leaks. But no water drip-drips this time through the window frame above the bookcase on the east wall, nor does it seep through the west wall onto the shag rug by the spare bedroom's door. The Chief has fought that floor-level leak with caulk and monumental cussing for years. Satisfied that he's finally waged a successful holding action, he comes to rest at the kitchen table with coffee and plans for building a boat ramp off our seawall. We might be better off if he were making plans to build an ark.

Watching him, I think of all the things I could be doing on this confining, gully-washing, cataractal day. I could read, write letters, knit, or make a fancy dinner, the kind that takes hours and many herbs to prepare. I could fold laundry—the basket of clean clothes holds three load's worth—or I could undertake a wrestling session with the house python, as the Chief has chosen to call our vacuum cleaner with the long hose that can coil around legs in an instant. Lord knows, we've tracked a Sahara of sand onto the shag rug and the kitchen linoleum. I choose instead to contemplate this streaming, soaking phenomenon for which the English language has a hundred words and none at all.

I do know some plain facts about rain. Today's rain is made of primeval water—water that has existed constantly and in the same quantity since molecules of oxygen and hydrogen collided and joined not long after the planet was formed. Earth's oldest oceans and its earliest rains are still with us, though their water has since appeared in myriad guises, from ice cap to bog, from snow to steam or invisible vapor. And water rolls on a great wheel called the hydrological cycle: evaporation, condensation, precipitation. This morning's downpour began in the clouds. Up there, dust specks and other infinitesimal bits of floating matter provided the nuclei needed for vapor to condense into minuscule droplets. Then the droplets merged, plumping out until they were heavy enough to fall without evaporating down to the earth, to the parched soil of Great Neck Point.

I also know things about rain that have nothing to do with the facts:

> *It's raining, it's pouring,*
> *The old man is snoring,*
> *Bumped his head and wet his bed*
> *And couldn't get up this morning.*

That's an American version of the childhood classic—the one learned at recess out of adult earshot. The more polite and continent old man endorsed by my parents simply went to bed. The verse that English children sing to the same "A-Tisket A-Tasket" tune ignores the old man and his doings altogether and compares the rain to pepper falling from a box "and all the little ladies are holding up their frocks."

The deluge slacks off. Chanting playground singsong, I open the back door to sniff the air and listen. What I get is a faceful of cool raindrops, the scent of wet earth, and not an old man's snoring but the whistles of bobwhite announcing their name and the briskly bugled chow-call song of the orchard orioles.

Some rains are not so benign—from the ancient sky-burst that sent Noah drifting across new-formed seas for forty days to the here-and-now downpours that do not cease for days on end but flood the Mississippi, break its levees, and drown not only the seeds just planted in the fields but a thousand thousand hopes and dreams. But today's rain is water from heaven. And, oh, we have needed it.

For the last three weeks, the world has been sweltering, the air holding its moisture-swollen breath. My grandmother, a mistress of the art of delicate speech, told me that horses sweat, men perspire, ladies glow— or "dreen," if they're old-fashioned South Carolina ladies, sitting on the porch swings drinking lemonade and gently fluttering their fans. In my grandmother's book, I'm a horse. Weeding the garden, walking, cooking, cleaning fish, working at any activity, I flat-out sweat. Not only do I soak the underarms of my shirt but the back and front as well. As for the Chief, his brow and upper lip become beaded as soon as he opens his mouth to talk. But we can endure the humid heat, can compensate by moving sluggishly, drinking gallons of iced tea, and showering away the sweated salt when darkness brings temperatures down from the high nineties to the comparatively arctic high seventies. And day or night, we can always plop our wilting bodies in the river.

The trees, however, have been coated with dust from the dirt lane. The garden has panted with thirst, and even prolonged watering with the sprinkler has not put the pep back into drooping bell peppers. Nor have the birds escaped punishment. The heat has made them silent and reclusive, hoarding their energy. Nor have they had ready sources of water for drinking and baths. Even the nearly everlasting puddle on the dirt lane has dried up. The birds were looking elsewhere for water—in buckets and barrels containing the algae-green remnants of past rains, in the river itself. Several mornings ago, a pair of cardinals chose the river for their ablutions. I saw the cock glide down to perch on the moving rim of a wave; the hen flew with him but caught herself in time and rose intact. Scarlet leaf bobbing on grey-brown water: The handle of our dip net was half a foot too short for me to reach him. I do not know if he was able to come ashore. Only the river's children seem to have fared well through these sultry weeks. Though superheated winds have desiccated the land, frequent southwesterly gusts have churned the water into oxygen-trapping whitecaps. There's been no fish-kill, with air-starved bodies floating on the surface. Instead, the finny creatures have been swimming all along into our nets, the blue crabs scuttling into our pots.

We deserve today's fat, juicy drops. For three weeks, we've been tantalized, grasping at storms that disappeared before they reached our shore. Late afternoons and evenings, thunderheads regularly built themselves over the river's far bank in tall, grey columns crowned with dazzling bursts of sunlight. Brilliant chains of lightning connected heaven and earth. Thunder followed like an old man's timber-shivering snores, like rumbling growls from some great Olympian gut. Or perhaps Zeus was laughing. Watching the storms roll out of reach, we sighed and sweated.

Today, no lightning slashes down, no thunder booms. I hear rain and the revitalized birds, not just bobwhite and orioles but bluebirds, cardinals, three kinds of warblers, and the cheerily loudmouthed wrens. Their wet feathers are plastered to their bodies, but they've waked from torpor, they're singing up a shivaree.

"Whee!" I holler back. My shirtfront is soaked this time with deliciously cool, clean water, not salty sweat. It's as if we walking, flying, wriggling, hopping creatures of the land have needed water-laden air as much as sea creatures need oxygen-laden water. Now we all celebrate the quenching of our heart's thirst. Drops pelt on the world like grains of rice flung at a bride and groom.

We're also celebrating something else, something primordial. Tomorrow, though I'll encumber myself with rubber boots to slog through puddles and the mud of the dirt lane, though the mosquitoes will be resurrected and thirsty, my shirt will stay dry. I'll smell newly cleansed air and see the bell peppers standing erect. Toads and frogs will croak in full, a cappella chorus. There may be a hatch of dragonflies. The birds will definitely put themselves on tuneful display. We've all been guests at a wedding—*hieros gamos*, the sacred marriage.

Twenty-five hundred years ago, the playwright Aeschylus saw moisture leached by hot winds from Greek soil. He saw rivers vanishing beneath their beds, plants withering, sheep and goats nibbling at parched vegetation, and human laborers sweating as profusely over dusty fields as warhorses in the dusty thick of battle. When at last the rains came, sweetening the land, filling streams, plumping out the flocks and their keepers, he listened to the primeval language of storms and translated it into his own tongue, his own understanding. And this is what Aeschylus heard and handed on.

In the final play of a prize-winning trilogy, the fifty daughters of Danaos plot at their father's behest to murder their fifty bridegrooms, brutal men, before the marriages can be consummated. One daughter, only one, looks on her new husband's face and chooses to think not of past violence but of future promise. She drops her knife. He lives. And she is tried for filial disobedience but exonerated because she has bowed to something more powerful than her father's wishes; she has honored a timeless and divine command. Aphrodite herself, the incarnation of re-alized sexuality, appears and blesses the couple's mortal marriage in terms of the eternal marriage from which all living things have sprung. The play is lost now except for the goddess's words and the recurrent miracle they praise:

> Desire   yes   Sky's holy quickfire longs
> to pierce the curvèd world
> Desire desire   grips Earth and reels her
> toward the coupling.
> And Sky's rain   showered in their blissful bed
> impregnates Earth
> and She gives birth   the herds' grass and the grain
> for man's joy and continuing.
> By that torrential wedding   life learns its seasons—
> the sprout, the flower, the completed fruit.
> And I within   am accomplice.

Today it's raining cats and dogs. It's pouring orioles and bluebirds, snapping turtles, lizards, pollywogs, and gallinippers. It's pouring butterflies, not to mention fire ants and ticks. It's pouring pines, live oaks, hickories, and holly, trumpet vines, honeysuckle, poison ivy, grass for Sally to roll on and the Chief to mow, weeds to be yanked from the garden, and dozens of sweet California Wonder bell peppers for me to stuff and freeze or put on the supper table. And people are flowering, bursting out of their tight, dry pods. We're waterstruck, all of us, and all of us are not only guests at the wedding but witnesses to its consummation. We're also sopping proof of the primal couple's measureless fertility.

"Whee!" Sally comes to the back door to see what I'm whooping about. She pokes her nose outside just long enough to get it splattered. She looks at me just long enough to tell me I'm crazy and walks primly back to the sofa. Well, she can snooze away this lusty, pelting weather. Her people won't. We owe this day our reverent jubilation.

ring-a-ring

o' roses

every May, roses surge up in a spring tide to inundate the uncared-for land just upstream from ours. The ground is awash with a blush-white foam, and cascades of pink and mauve spill down to the river over a five-foot cliff of severely eroded clay. The weedy, thorny tangles of the place, the decaying trees felled by storms and high water, the overgrown and disintegrating trailers are beautifully flooded. Then, after three weeks, the tide recedes, leaving no obvious signs that it had ever swept in. And these events occur so quietly that it took my brain nine slow years to notice what I'd been seeing all along.

Where did they come from, these little roses? How did they get here? Of the world's many roses, what kind are they? Nothing like them appears on the pages of my wildflower guides.

On the theory that knowledge begins with observation, I look at the roses and look again. They neither climb nor grow upright but hug the ground, sprawling luxuriantly in both the sunny spaces and the dim green shadows. The flowers, hardly more than an inch across, bloom in clusters, and the petals of each blossom spread as full and ruffled as a flounce of petticoats. But these roses do not sweeten the air; the only scent that I can sniff out is a faint, green, generic sort of freshness. The canes, lithe and slender as vines, bear thorns all right, but with such modesty that my exploring fingers are never in danger of being pricked.

Brave roses not to retreat or turn brown in the river's salt-rich air. Stubborn roses to bloom triumphant every year amid broken glass, decaying wood, and a jungle of rapacious weeds. Generous roses to give their vitality to a run-down wreck of a place that is owned but not cherished. What are these roses, anyway?

My neighbor Eva might know. Her large tribe, now much dispersed, has lived variously at Great Neck Point on the wide and salty river Neuse for six generations. But, always vague and dismissive about the old days, she's not a likely source of information. And I can tell by looking at her yard that she's not a gardener. Her taste in decorative outdoor greenery runs to volunteer mimosa trees and hanging baskets of spider plants, begonias, and ivy.

What *are* these roses? A curiosity that just won't quit pushes me to the telephone. Any plans I may have made for the afternoon vanish the instant the proprietor of a greenhouse and nursery business suggests that I snip some blossoms and bring them in. "Need to see them to identify them," he says, and instructs me to put the samples in a zip-tight plastic bag. The roses and I are in his salesroom nearly an hour later—five minutes to snip and bag the cuttings, forty-five minutes to drive up the road. Though he's our nearest nurseryman, his nearness is relative and yet another illustration of the plain country fact that no commercial enterprise is truly close to our tucked-away rural enclave on the east bank of the Neuse.

"Older variety of cultivated rose," he says, turning the bag this way and that. Several customers come over to see what he's looking at, and he uses the occasion to treat us all to a short educational talk. "They root real easily, roses like this. After frost, that's when you root them. Put them in a box with a mix of peat moss and perlite. Now look here—you see this?" He points to a cluster of tightly closed buds.

I ask what I'm supposed to see.

"Why you needed to use a bag—the necks of the buds, look, powdery mildew."

I appreciate his caution—no sense infecting his own stock. I hadn't noticed the coating of fine silver dust where the buds attach to the stem and, even if I had, couldn't have put a name to it. Now I know and won't forget. But there's another question of identity in which I'm far more interested. "Can you tell me what kind of roses these roses are?"

"Can't put a name to them," he says.

"They remind me of something, I can't remember what," says a middle-aged woman who's been looking and listening.

"Can tell you, though," he says, "this is a species cultivated back in the '30s."

My hopes aren't entirely dashed. I've learned two things. One is that these are tough little roses to flourish despite a fungal disease that would do in their less thrifty cousins. The other has to do with cultivation: These roses are tame! Somebody planted them. Not only that, but planted them sixty-odd years ago.

"I've got it!" the middle-aged woman exclaims. "They look rather like the Fairy rose. I ordered one of those from Wayside Gardens ten, twelve years ago. Once it starts blooming, it just doesn't stop."

The nursery man nods in assent. Thanking him, away I go.

Fairy—that's a varietal name, like Peace, Blaze, or Dolly Parton, and pictures in the Wayside catalogue at home show fluffy pink rosettes clustered in such profusion that they almost obscure the plant's green leaves. Growing on upright canes, flowering successively from early summer till frost, they are most definitely not the recumbent Maytime rose next door.

But never mind. Can it be that the roses blooming in the unkempt wilderness next door are guarding a secret? The notion takes root and grows, leafing out, budding, beginning to flower, and all because a word has gone spinning through air like a seed. And I find that I am spun into a magical place in which everyday reality becomes a fertile ground for fairy tales. Here anything might sprout up, from brambles to bean stalks. Here, in all likelihood, for more than half a century a thick, briery tangle of roses has stood watch over someone sound asleep. In this particular unfolding of the ancient tale, her name is Blossom. She shall be castled in rose-guarded darkness for one hundred years, give birth as she sleeps to twin children, Sun and Moon, and sleep on, not heeding the babies' cries. No, she will keep on dreaming the dream that imprisons her, a dream of girlhood never coming to fruit, forever safe from blood drawn by a thorn or a king's rape. Hunting, he'd been led by frightened prey through woods where the oak trees moved aside to ease his way, briers parted, and the castle gates unlocked themselves to let him enter. As soon as he had slaked his lust on flesh willing only to sleep, he rode away, forgetting Blossom's beauty. Many seasons later, when a hunt in the same woods stirs his memory, he shall find his own Sun and Moon rising together, their radiance reflected in their mother's opened eyes. But when he returns to his palace with the scent of roses on him, and the animal musk of children, jealousy shall strike his lady-queen. Without his knowledge, she shall command Sun and Moon to a banquet and order a fire so that they, their lives extinguished, may be perfectly served to their faithless father. Two lambs shall be slaughtered instead, and the children hidden so that they may live. It is they, after all, who have cleansed their mother of dreams. There is no pretty kiss to figure in her wakening. There never was nor shall be. No, it's the tugging of newborn hunger at Blossom's breasts, and with each tug a contraction, sharp as a necessary thorn, to knit the stretched womb. And the instant that Blossom opens her eyes and reaches full flower, the roses shall bloom more fragrant and joyful than ever before.

But as this tale is told, Blossom is still in her tight little bud, pregnant with possibilities but sound asleep. She's not due to wake for another forty years. Hidden in darkness, guarded by roses, several small lives are taking form. Over there behind a tumble of May-blooming roses, look! There, in the rusty clay of the riverbank, about four feet above the water—a burrow. Its mouth gapes like an *oh* of surprise. I wouldn't have known the hole was a burrow, wouldn't have seen it in the first place, without the pair of swallows leading my eye.

Northern rough-wingeds, that's what they are—small, brown, graceful birds that can turn on a mote of sunlight. Chittering, they sweep the air or skim the water snapping up insects and—blip—disappear amid roses. Now that it's May, they're nesting. They didn't excavate the burrow but have simply claimed it and lined its damp interior with pine straw as a bed for six or seven glossy white eggs. Likely, the burrow has been there for years, dug by a small mammal—mouse, vole, rabbit?—that started tunneling toward the river from some point inland. This spring the swallows have been well served by neglect. To their great good fortune, the owner of the place has not held it in high enough regard to protect it with a seawall. And year after year, under the recurrent lash of northeast winds, the water has reared up and clawed away such chunks of its bank that the riverward end of the tunnel is now exposed.

Neglect? Lunacy! The place covered more than eight acres when the man who owns it purchased it in 1980, before I'd ever heard of the river Neuse. For nine years now I've lived on its eastern shore—a long time to look at little roses without once seeing them. But I have seen all along, from my first day on the river, the wasting away of the land next door. It shrinks before our eyes, eight acres eroded to a scant four. The footpath that followed the shore upriver to the creek and a sandy beach—a route well-used by people, dogs, and white-tailed deer—is five years gone. The Chief and I scramble to save our land. At its upriver end, our bulkhead turns inland at a right angle, and we keep extending this wing-wall—fifty feet, twenty-five more feet, and another twenty-five—to prevent the retreat of his shoreline from dragging ours with it.

Is he aware of the roses? I doubt it. He visits seldom, perhaps no more than once a year, and when he does come, he pauses, intent and scowling, for only an hour. The apparition of surveyors, though never from the same firm, is the greatest indication of his continuing interest in the place. Every eighteen months or so, a new team goes to work, slashing alleys through the underbrush and tying electric-pink plastic ribbons to every old concrete survey monument and iron stake they can find. Sometimes, after one of these incursions, a fence has gone up, twice cutting across the neat field of the neighbor just inland from the tangled mess and once, good grief, slicing from back line to seawall right through our yard. We were elsewhere at the time, but when neighbors called to sound a red alert, the Chief lost not a minute rushing back to remove it. The theory behind such fences is that deeds to the river lots specify dimensions not only in degrees of latitude and longitude but also in feet—so many feet in this direction, so many in that. And if the river claims the land, then some ignoramuses (though not the surveyors) think it quite proper to move a boundary up, down, or inland so that the loss is replaced with the requisite number of deed-sanctioned feet.

It's easy to come to grips, though, with fences that spring up in the wake of a survey. They're nothing but weeds of human devising, and we can root them out. What we can't do is bring back land that somebody else let slide most wantonly into the river's long and ever-greedy gut. I'm half in rage about this ruination.

And half not. When it comes to the acres not yet devoured by the river, neglect spins around 180 degrees to show a benign side. There's much to be said in favor of leaving the wild world to its own natural devices. For starters, the dainty, May-blooming roses ramble where they will and flourish. Marching through waist-high grass, through creepers and briars, skirting the myrtle bushes and sweet gum saplings, they grow right up to our yard, and there they stop short, refraining from any trespass whatsoever across the boundary line. Clearly, they prefer a tangled mess to the less catastrophic untidiness that we offer them. I'm the one who trespasses, invading their territory almost every day. The same see-nothing, do-nothing ignorance that benefits roses benefits me: I've nothing to fear. A man who doesn't bother to visit can't possibly catch me at my misdemeanors.

Why prowl through his thickety underbrush? Why risk thorns and poison ivy, ticks, chiggers, and snakes? For roses, certainly, and rough-winged swallows. For the wild clematis called leather flower, with inch-long, bell-shaped lavender blossoms, that's supposed to grow up in the mountains but not, for heaven's sake, down here in the sand and salt spray. For the sheer delight of discovering other such wonders amid the general mess, which qualifies as a mess only in human terms. Now that the water has taken the footpath along the riverbank, hardly anyone bothers to look at the place, much less invade it. The pleasure of its use reverts to the wild creatures, and I sneak in to watch.

Slider turtles rise out of the water, herons stalk the shore, and river otters play, while osprey and sometimes bald eagles cry overhead. Pileated woodpeckers drill nest cavities in pine snags; flickers or squirrels occupy the holes the following year. Warblers pause in the dense woods during migration. A swarm of bees hangs in a live oak; the wriggling, whining mass is bigger that a football. Deer browse in the overgrown clearing. Foxes pass through, and bobcats. Once I saw the footprints of a bear. The birds and animals seem to know that the two derelict trailers house no threat to their well-being.

These trailers would be eyesores if not for the screening vegetation—
shrubs grown higher than the windows, vines curling over the roofs. Not
long after the present (and notably absent) owner bought the place in
1980, he brought in the newer, larger trailer—a blue, two-bedroom mo-
bile home—and set it down at woods' edge near the back property line.
But he put a heavy padlock on the main door and never, that we know of,
spent a single night within. It has been the scene, though, of unautho-
rized shenanigans. Someone smashed through the back door, and I remember that the trailer rocked and rolled for two or three years with
parties that the teenaged perpetrators wouldn't have been allowed to
hold at home.

The other trailer, which began its career as a travel camper, is older
and seedier, a remnant of the late '50s. That's the era in which the eight-
plus acres were originally detached from the farm belonging to my
neighbor Eva's family, who had raised crops of corn and tobacco here
since before the turn of the century. In the '50s, a sandy beach still
stretched along the shore, and the people who'd bought the place as a
weekend retreat pulled in the camper. They tacked on a large wooden
porch, built a pier and a fish-cleaning table, dug a well, and brought in
an old school bus for use as a guest house. For the next couple of decades,
they tamed the place and tended it. When I came on the scene, the
school bus had disappeared, but wilderness had only begun its en-
croachment. Ten years later, the porch is all cattywampus; the camper's
windows are broken out, its kitchen counter charred where vandals set
fires. It harbors refuse and Carolina wrens. One pier piling, barnacled
and worm-eaten, still stands upright, but the cleaning table was shot to
pieces when neighborhood young'uns set bottles and cans on its surface
and used them for target practice. The well pipe, on land when I first saw
it, juts out of the water a good ten feet offshore.

Amid this exuberant ruin, little roses. I ask the Chief to take photographs so that we'll have proof of these unlikely blossoms after they've
withered and disappeared. If the nurseryman is right, that they belong to

the '30s, then they were blooming here at least two decades before the weekend people arrived on the river. Did the weekenders see the roses and rejoice? Did they cut clusters of flowers and put them in a jelly jar to decorate the kitchen counter? Or did the roses, avoiding lawn mowers and trampling feet, slip modestly out of the way? If that's the case, where could they have gone? Out of sight, out of mind.

The roses bloom right merrily in the river version of a very old tale. And most of the major characters are already on the scene—black bear at the edge of the clearing, live oak in the deep woods, stingray in the wide and salty river, bald eagle in the high blue air. And the two girls are here as well—tall, slender Palustris and her daintier sister Carolina. Palustris prefers the moist, sun-dappled shadows beneath the trees, while Carolina thrives in open fields and full golden sunlight. Both girls are as blushing and shy as the wild roses, the swamp rose and the pasture rose, for which they were named. The necessary dwarf is also present, but should he try sneaking off, the magic of stories will instantly seize him by the scruff—unlike his cousin in the traditional tale, this dwarf has no beard—and haul him back here where he belongs. The only character not immediately on hand is the girls' mother, but I'll step into her role, which is that of a bystander who observed what happened and now makes a report.

Today, Palustris and Carolina are on their own, living in a palace full of shaggy black bears. But that's now. Time was that the three of us lived not in the hut you may have heard about but in an old camping trailer with a wooden porch tacked on. Clusters of May-blooming roses, blush-white to mauve, planted when the girls were babies, covered the earth near the porch steps.

In spring, summer, and fall, those girls rarely stayed home. They were off finding wild honey in the woods, catching blue crabs down at the creek, and making friends with all the animals. The cottontails nibbled leaves right out of their hands, deer browsed beside them, nor did the shy catbirds and thrashers hide at their approach but perched in the open and sang every song they could invent. Best of all, the dolphins out in the river gave them leaping, splashing rides. Nothing ever harmed those girls, not poison ivy, not ticks, not the copperheads that sometimes lie concealed under the deadfalls in the woods nor the stingrays lurking on the river's sandy bottom.

In winter, however, the girls kept close to my woodstove. That stove was especially cozy four years ago when the temperature plummeted to zero right after Christmas. The wide and salty river froze clear across, all five miles of it, and snow fell for two days straight, drifting up to four feet in the back fields. The blizzard began to taper off after dark on the second day, and we'd just finished supper when somebody thumped on the door. Turned out to be a big black hogbear—a he-bear, that is, as distinct from a female or sow. As he lumbered inside, he said that he wouldn't hurt us and asked most politely if we'd remove the painful iceballs that had formed between his toes. Of course, the girls obliged. Then the bear curled up under the kitchen table and stayed there till spring. Not a convenient place to hibernate, but the girls told me, "Leave him alone, Ma, he needs his sleep." When he woke, he growled something about having to guard his treasures from a thievish dwarf, and off he went.

The next part of the story is hearsay. I simply relate what the girls told me. By purest chance, they encountered the dwarf three times that summer. I haven't seen them since they left home the morning of the third encounter, but they did send an airmail message telling of that final episode.

The first time they saw him, the girls had heard a far-off scream for help and followed the wild, untoward sound deep into the woods. And there he was, halfway up a honey tree and covered from his bald spot to his bare feet with whining, stinging bees. The girls called off the bees, of course, but if they'd expected thanks, none were forthcoming. Instead, the dwarf cussed them up and down for losing him his honey. And he sidled away as quickly as a copperhead, but not before grabbing up a sack that looked as if it were filled with bright new hardware for a fence.

The second encounter took place on the river, where the girls had set a gill net to catch summer flounder. When they went to fish it, it was plain from the rapid bobbing of the net's corkline that something large was caught below the surface of the water. This time the dwarf, intending to rob the net, had found a stingray entangled in the meshes, and the energetic thrashing of the great winged fish had wrapped the net around the would-be robber. The venomous barb on its whiplike tail was perilously close to the dwarf's nose. The girls cut him loose, of course. This time he cussed them backwards and forwards for interfering with his research into marine biology. And he scuttled away like a blue crab, but not before grabbing up another sack that seemed to be filled with gleaming fence posts.

The third time, trouble struck from the air. At least, that's the direction from which it descended on the dwarf. The girls did not come home that day, but the eagle saw fit to bring me the news. This time, the girls came upon the dwarf as they crossed the back field on their way to a blackberry patch. At that moment, like a thunderbolt out of a blue sky, the eagle stooped, seized the dwarf in his talons, and would have carried him away except that Carolina hauled out her Swiss Army knife and cut the dwarf free. His jacket was all the eagle carried off. That dwarf cussed the girls upside down and sideways for spoiling his clothes. And he grabbed up a sack that appeared to hold a roll of shiny chain-link fence.

At this point in the story, the bear is supposed to show up, kill the dwarf who'd put him under an evil spell, and turn into a true, blue-blooded prince. That's not what happened. The bear arrived on cue all right— two bears, in fact, for his brother came with him. Ignoring the dwarf, those beasts kidnapped my daughters—took them off to a palace in the mountains. Or my daughters call it a palace in the letters they write home, but the way the eagle describes the place, it's really a big cave. And that damnable dwarf is still down here on the river. He's taken to throwing great chunks of land into the water. The yard disappears, the shore comes ever closer to the porch, the enchanting roses bloom on.

That is, they bloom in the Chief's photographs. With the coming of June, the flowers vanish almost overnight. All that's left are the lacy dark-green leaves, and these are visible among rambunctious weeds and leaping vines only if you know to look for them in the first place.

The questions pricked by the roses become as insistent as the weeds. What kind of roses? And how did they get to this place on the riverbank? The nurseryman has supplied a single fact, that they are a cultivated variety. The blossoms of wild roses never exhibit such flounces and frills. But popular in the '30s? That statement sounds like educated speculation. The first question may be more amenable to finding a definitive answer, for it lies within the province of people who specialize in roses. A letter describing the flowers and their habitat goes off to the American Rose Society. Some of the Chief's photographs go with it.

Rosarians don't dillydally. A handwritten reply comes posthaste from the society's vice president. He is gracious but regretful that he cannot identify my "found" rose amid a difficult array of possibilities. He has, however, sent my inquiry and the photos along to someone who may indeed be able to help.

Waiting, I read about roses: that fossils forty million years old, from Japan, the United States, and several European countries, show leaves, twigs, and thorns that are clearly identifiable as belonging to the genus *Rosa*; that roses originated only in the northern hemisphere, and no native species has ever been found in any region south of the equator. Roses bloom amid iris and lilies in the murals of Knossos in Crete. Homer records in the *Iliad* that Hector's torn body, dragged around the walls of Troy, was anointed with rose oil before it was buried. In Rome, gardeners urged roses into winter bloom by growing them in greenhouses—and were railed at by the statesman and tragic playwright Seneca for turning nature upside down.

And I beguile myself with roses in other incarnations. Rose window, compass rose—how easily they lend their form and name to other ob-

jects! And how readily the poets turn roses to their own uses: Shake-
speare's rose by any other name; Yeats's "Far-off, most secret, and invio-
late Rose"; Gertrude Stein's self-defining, self-perpetuating "Rose is a rose
is a rose is a rose"; and Theodore Roethke's rose, the closest of all to the
roses by the river. He rejoices in much—in being himself, in lilacs, in
calm, in a bird,

> *And in this rose, this rose in the sea-wind,*
> *Rooted in stone, keeping the whole of light,*
> *Gathering to itself sound and silence—*
> *Mine and the sea-wind's.*

A letter arrives from the president of the Heritage Rose Foundation, a
group devoted to the care and preservation of roses that originated in the
nineteenth century. No, the little roses on the riverbank are not that old,
nor can he name their variety, but he tells me this: "The rose in your photographs is a Rambler, specifically a derivative of *Rosa wichuraiana*, which
is native to Japan. This species was first used in breeding about the turn
of the century and many hybrids like your rose were produced. Perhaps
the most famous one was 'Dorothy Perkins,' introduced in 1901."

I am gloriously satisfied. Along with its wild Asiatic forebear, the variety Dorothy Perkins is frequently pictured in books about roses. And
the little roses on the river so closely resemble Dorothy Perkins that only
a literalist would want to quibble. It could be that they arrived here not
in the '30s but earlier, much earlier, by a decade or three. How much at
home they've made themselves, these hardy river roses, snugged into the
sand and clay, bathed in the salt air, blooming year in, year out, as if
there'd never been a world without them, a world without any roses at
all, except for the one rose that waited in deep stillness under the sea—
imagine that! Ancient legends attested to this phenomenon, and the
Greek poet Pindar, picking up such reports, made them into a song that

celebrates to this day a boxing victory twenty-five hundred years ago in the Olympian Games. The champion came from the island of Rhodes—Rose Island.

But once upon a time so primeval that it is remembered only in stories—when Zeus and the other immortals cast lots to apportion the earth among themselves—Rose Island was not yet visible upon the surface of the sea but lay hidden in the deeps. As it happened, one who should have been there—Helios the Sun—was absent, and no one assigned him anything, though he was certainly a god. When he mentioned this oversight, Zeus offered to cast the lots a second time. "Don't," said the Sun. "Down there, on the seabed under the white-maned waves, I see something budding, wanting to sprout—a land to nurture people and give sweet pasture to their flocks. Award me that, and swear you'll never take it back once it lifts into the brilliant air." That's what he asked for, and that's what he got. Out of the salt sea an island rose, grew into the light, and bloomed. The Sun embraced his sea-born Rose with shining rays and lay with her and fathered seven boys, who are said to have been impressively bright.

Legend and Pindar say nothing of their girls, but I'm sure that there were daughters, each of them a rose, quiet but prickly, daughters indeed, an astonishment of daughters! The overgrown clearing, in which the river roses open themselves every May to the sun, once held a farmhouse, and in that house, Clara, Mary, and Eva lived with their parents. Their little sister Gwen was born in one of its bedrooms.

"Those roses? Those little brambly things grow all over the place?" Eva says when I finally talk with her. "Weeds! They are nothing but weeds."

But I don't talk with Eva at first, don't even think about going to see her, even after I find the other tame plants. It's Gwen who points me in Eva's direction, but more about that later.

Finding the plants is fortuitous, a by-product of efforts to blaze a rough trail through the woods to the creek and the sandy beach upriver.

Birds—gulls, herons, egrets, migrating plovers, and sandpipers and, once, a nearly miraculous pair of red-necked phalaropes—congregate on the creek's sandbars year-round. It used to be easy to sneak close to watch them, ten seconds to grab the binoculars and three minutes to dash along the shore-hugging footpath. But since the river sapped the land and took the path, reaching the creek has ceased to be a quick, simple matter. It calls for putting on river clothes to slosh through the water or making a twelve-minute walk inland across a neighbor's yard and then to the creek by way of an old, overgrown fence line that runs through a tunnel of trees. What a nuisance! So, I pick up clippers and hawksbill shears to make me a new, more direct route along the riverbank. But deadfalls and vines tied in Gordian knots obstruct the shoreline; only a chain saw can clear a path close to the water. So I start clipping through the underbrush near the upriver end of the larger trailer.

Look at that—Spanish bayonet! And not just one plant but two, growing right here in the woods. The long, tapered leaves are so stiff they might have been starched, and each leaf narrows to a needle-sharp point that can pierce flesh so painlessly that the wound isn't noticed until one's clothes are soaked with blood. It's one of the yuccas—*Yucca aloifolia* to be exact, which is not an everyday sight along the river. The yucca common here is beargrass, *Y. filamentosa*, with curly white threads springing from the raveled edges of its leaves. It grows wild everywhere. The low tufts, lush as chenille, thrive in the sand at the creek and thrust up, despite repeated mowing, amid the grass in our yard. But Spanish bayonet? I've never seen it in these parts except as an ornamental. Yet here, in the shadowy woods, are two of them, nor did they get here by themselves. Somebody planted them, but not recently, for both are as tall as my shoulders and have trunks as stout as my legs. It strikes me that they might be standing sentinel, guarding the roses. Then I pick up clippers and shears and eventually work my way through to the creek.

As it turns out, the rambler roses and the serendipitous Spanish bayonet are not the only cultivated plants to which I've been shamefully blind.

Other tame species have not only persisted but flourished, long after being abandoned by the people who set them in the earth. For years,
though its flowers of periwinkle blue are as big around as quarters, I've
overlooked a sprawl of *Vinca major* behind the larger trailer. Till now, I
haven't really registered the sight of white flowers, abundant in April, that
rise from clumps of slender, dark-green leaves and dangle, several to a
stem, like little bells. My field guide to domesticated plants, the Wayside
Gardens catalogue, identifies them as *Leucojum vernum*, more commonly
known as spring snowflake. It describes them, with copywriter's hyperbole, as "very rare." And without taking note of the source of the fragrance, I've paused in my tracks to sniff the sweet and heady air in late
May when several small trees come into bloom—*Ligustrum sinense*, Chinese
privet. This far south, it keeps its large, glossy leaves all winter long.
Though the plant, naturalized since its introduction from China, spreads
without human help, it often marks the sites of former human habita-
tion—both the houses and the hands that planted the privet decades
gone.

And there are the gladioli, lifting their green swords in May, blooming through June and July—dozens and dozens of gladioli, all of them
red. Not another color in the lot, just red: the red of a summer tanager's
feathers; the red of a sweet, sun-ripened tomato; red-hot chile pepper
red. I have noticed *them*, of course. Who could miss that brash, incendiary brightness amid the weeds and vines next door? Self-seeding, spreading themselves like wildfires, they blaze in our yard too. People living at
the Point dig up the winter-hardy corms for planting in their own gardens. I'd somehow thought, without really thinking at all, that these
glads were wild, never mind that glads do not appear in wildflower
guides. They're tame, of course, and like the roses and the Spanish bayonet, the privet and the periwinkle, they came here by human design to
grace a garden or kept-up yard. And they're tough as the roses, able to
snuggle in and thrive without human care. But unlike their more modest
companions, the glads red-flag the attention of everyone passing by.

Now dispersed around the Point by wind and trowel, they still cluster thickest where first they were planted next door.

The mystery starts to come clear when I pause on the way back from our distant mailbox to chat with Eva's sister Gwen. We get to talking about storms and high water and how much land the river has taken.

"Yeah, the place next door to you, shame what's happening to it. I was born there," Gwen says. A fourth-generation member of the prodigious tribe that farmed this land for nearly a hundred years, well into the 1970s, she lives in New Jersey these days but comes to the Point and stays in her trailer just inland from the river for six weeks every summer. "My mama and daddy, they were living right there in the farmhouse at that time. Of course, the land went a lot farther out in the river back then."

I've known Gwen for a decade, but this is the first I've heard of a farmhouse on that piece of property. The homestead the tribe always talks about, a two-story structure seen by many of the outlanders living here now, was situated near the Point end, not the creek end, of the farm. When a storm-surge of high water ruined the downstairs, the family's matriarch and her husband moved upstairs for a while, then built a new house and let the old one tumble down. But a farmhouse next door to my yard? Today, there's not one trace of such a building. Eagerly I inquire about the particulars.

But Gwen says that she doesn't remember the house at all, she was just a baby. "And when I got old enough to remember things, it wasn't there."

"Wasn't there?"

"Oh yes, it got all blown to hell and gone in the hurricane of '33. You've heard about that hurricane, chickens forty feet up in the trees and the cows swimming through the woods. That's the year I was born."

That's my year, too, but I don't tell her so right away. A farmhouse! That's an excellent reason for someone, perhaps Gwen's mother, to plant blushing roses and red, red glads to make the dooryard pretty. But when I ask Gwen who built the farmhouse and how long it had stood on the site before the hurricane battered it down, she says that she has no idea and suggests that her sister Eva might know. Eva, after all, is several years older.

But Eva, who lives year-round amid the spider plants and begonias in a three-bedroom, three-bath double-wide down near the mailboxes, does not recall the house nor living there and has never bothered to wonder who might have built it. Only the roses stayed in her mind. When she became a wife and mother, she remembered them as pretty, dug some up, planted them in her own yard, and watched them take over, insistent and grabby as a headstrong child. Now, when I ask if her mother might have been the one who first planted the little old-fashioned ramblers at Great Neck Point, she snorts, "Huh! Weeds!" Nonetheless, even though I get no direct information from Eva, she does impart a modicum of tribal history. A bare genealogical outline, really, but it's enough to satisfy my curiosity about the roses.

Some people shrug off the past the way a butterfly slits and sheds its chrysalis. And it need not be a matter of leaving physical or psychic pain behind, but just the casting off of something perceived as a terrible embarrassment—in this case, scratch-dirt poverty. It doesn't count that overcoming adversity is an integral part of the great American Horatio Alger success story. Such embarrassment, however unreasoned, acts as a true impediment to memory. I've seen this phenomenon time and again. And memory's response is that of the deserted chrysalis: It shrivels up and blows away.

What follows, then, are not the facts but surmises based on slender clues. The farmhouse taken by the legendary hurricane of '33 was built in the late 1800s by Gwen and Eva's great-grandparents, John and Mary Grover, who came across the river with their three little girls to take up farming, blacksmithing, and brick making at Great Neck Point. At that time, the Point lay at the nether end of a rough dirt road and sent its crops to market by boat. My imagination, however, doesn't see Mary Grover as the woman who planted the roses, for they represent a type of rambler developed around the turn of the century, well after she and

John arrived here. I think it was their daughter Carrie, married in 1901 at the age of thirteen, living with her young husband under the parental roof, whose hands dug a rose bed, tucked in the rootlets and stems, and patted the earth firm around them. And I nominate Carrie as the one most likely to have gussied up the place patriotically with gladiolus red, spring-snowflake white, and periwinkle blue. (It was certainly Carrie who much later moved upstairs in the other farmhouse after high water spread muck and other ruination all over the downstairs.)

Surmise draws a blank on the next two and a half decades, except for the fact that the smithy and the brickworks ceased operations. The farmhouse and its roses come into focus again in the late '20s, when Carrie's only living daughter, Lena, and her husband Henry moved in. Henry, a feckless charmer whose eyes were periwinkle blue, worked sometimes at the sawmill trade, sometimes as a tenant farmer, and not infrequently as a driver running moonshine over the state line to Virginia. Lena eventually gave him thirteen children, of whom a full dozen survived into adulthood. (That's a recipe right there for scratch-dirt poverty.) But in 1932, the year before the hurricane, they had four children, one son and three daughters, with Gwen on the way. It's the girls I see—Clara, Mary, and Eva, little girls, and they're racing around the yard on a sweet May afternoon. One of them, only a toddler, staggers and squeals as she tries to keep up with her not-much-bigger sisters. The squeals turn to shrieks when she falls into the thorny patch of roses rambling beside the porch steps. Wiping flour off her hands, mama runs out of the house to see what the bloody-murder noise is all about. Then she smiles, comforts her baby, and decides that making the supper biscuits can wait. She'll show her little girls a game:

> *Ring-a-ring o' roses,*
> *A pocket full of posies,*
> *A-tishoo! A-tishoo!*
> *We all fall down.*

Around, around, around they go, mother and little girls. They fall and rise and fall and finally lie right there on the ground laughing. But mama knows it's time to cut those roses back again. They're pretty things but bad as brambles, always out of hand.

And still they ramble here, there, everywhere just as they please! Nothing yet has kept those roses within any bounds. Likely, nothing will. They'll endure while everything else around here insists on falling down—houses, trees, piers, waterfront land and, along with these, our aspirations and our very lives. Faithfully obeying the circle of the seasons year after year, they form their own ring—bloom, retreat, and bloom again. And in the ring of roses, everything connects with everything else—land with water, fairy tales with fact, today with yesterday and to-morrow.

Every May the roses surge up in a spring tide, the ground is awash with their blush-white foam, and cascades of pink and mauve spill down to the river.

who has seen
the wind?

a northerly wind was gusting hard this morning when I drove off on a grocery run to town. It blew pine straw across the empty yard; it slapped water against the bulkhead and shook the sweet gum leaves like castanets. This afternoon a new din has been added to the wind-created uproar. The yard is mobbed.

Youngsters of junior-high-school age, a couple dozen of them, male and female, swarm laughing and hollering over the grass by the bulk-head. Three sit rocking in the cedar swing. Two more teeter in the rope hammock; one falls to the ground, and the other shouts, "Ha ha!" Our dog Sally is having a fine time romping from one group to another, wag-ging not just her tail but her whole rump and reveling in the attention she's being given. She doesn't notice, doesn't care how utterly bizarre these young'uns look. They wear conventional shorts, sneakers, and wa-terproof yellow jackets, but Hallowe'en designs decorate their faces—clowns, Indians, pouting dolls, monsters from outer space. These days, protective sunscreens come in as many colors as greasepaint. But it's not sunny today. Who are these gaudy and pubescent party-goers? How did they get here? Where did they come from? What *has* the Chief been up to in my absence?

"Hi," the mob choruses as I leave the car. One asks, "Are you Mrs. Chief?"

The Chief himself pops out of our trailer. "Hon, come in and meet some people. I'll get the groceries in a minute."

More people? Yes. Two young men and two young women sit at the kitchen table. The sun has bleached their hair and eyebrows and tinted their skins various shades from bronze to raw pink. The young woman with freckles sports a peeling nose.

"Port in a storm," the Chief says. "It's sort of an emergency."

"And sort of not, not now anyway," says one of the young men. "The kids are safe. We've got the boats secured. Hey, please don't tell 'em I'm in here smoking." He's also drinking a can of the Chief's beer.

We have a ruckus of castaways marooned in our yard—campers and counselors from one of the sailing camps directly across the river. The camp's boats give us a summer-long, if inadvertent, show of snowy sails gleaming against the pine-dark land and the shiny grey-brown water. This morning, the counselor-captains and the crew of swabbies now in our yard had boarded a fleet of twenty-foot Flying Scots and hoisted sail. The order of the day: to cruise five miles downriver, visit the historic fishing community on the same shore as the camp, and sail back home before evening chow call. They hadn't considered the wind. As soon as the sails were up, wind bellied them out with a thump and shoved the tiny boats out from shore at a right angle to the course that had been planned. It shoved them clear across the heaving, whitecapped river. The only part of the voyage that conformed to the original intent was the five-mile distance from port to port. The fleet had homed in on the beach near Courts Creek, but the Chief had seen them coming and hallooed them toward the more civilized haven of our yard. The boats I hadn't noticed on my arrival are tied to stumps on the eroded shore immediately upriver from our place. Sails furled, they huddle there as white and helpless as penned sheep.

Every year, wind rearranges the plans of people who ply the river in boats. More quickly than an owl can swivel its head, wind will shift 180 degrees. Faster than Proteus, old man of the sea, could change himself from lion to serpent to rushing water, the wind transforms itself from mild southerly breeze to a blast from the north. It may bring torrents of rain or hit as a dry hurricane that sends local anemometers to the eighty-mile top of their scale. Either way, the wind-driven water rises, wearing a frenzied lather of whitecaps. Waves lash at the shore and roll over the tops of our bulkheads. Every year boats are hurled off course to fetch up on our shore, to run aground as often as not on the sandbar at the mouth of Courts Creek.

Nor are we safe who plant our feet on solid ground. On one recent September night, as everyone in our neighborhood cleaned fish and a boat chugged out to bring ashore the last gill net, the wind hauled—BOOM! It was that sudden, that loud, the shift from steady, summer-warm southeasterlies to an arctic punch out of the north. The river's wind-pushed water rose a foot and a half in two minutes; the temperature dropped twenty degrees. Cold front slamming in, but it felt like an earthquake. The world shook and kept shaking. Knives rattled and danced, headless fish skittered across the cleaning tables. Sheared-off pine branches battered us like billy clubs. Guarding bloody blades and carcasses between our arms, we clung for dear life to the shuddering tables. Gill net abandoned to the gale, the boat turned shoreward and headed into the wind. Waves slapped over her bow, and she took on water nearly enough to sink her before she struggled to a mooring at our pier. The wind released the people cleaning fish—after how long? Fifteen eternal minutes? Only five? The boat was not quite so fortunate. Waves bashed her against pilings, and the bolts attaching pier-runners to the pilings holed her just under the starboard gunwale. In the night, after we'd all stumbled inside, wind-abetted water lifted her mooring lines off the pilings and flung her upriver into the grip of a fallen tree. That tree was a blessing; if she'd gone farther upriver, drowned and jagged stumps would have clawed her hull apart. Next morning, the river still savage, she was rescued, water-laden but still afloat.

How strong was that wind when it struck? The Point's educated opinion puts its speed at fifty knots. By comparison, we find no terror in the not-so-stiff nor'westerly breeze that has filled our yard with camper-castaways.

Wind is Great Neck Point's constant companion. It, more than water, seems the sternest elemental force with which we must reckon. Christina Rossetti's poem asks, "Who has seen the wind?" and immediately answers, "Neither I nor you." Eyes witness only its deeds: pollen or forest-fire smoke blown in thick, horizontal drifts; soil gouged away by wind-impelled water; shoreside pines and live oaks and cypresses undermined and toppled; the water's downstream flow reversed and the water level rising relentless as a spring tide. The wind makes its appearance not to sight but to the other senses. It brings to our noses the perfume of honeysuckle or the stench of decaying weeds and dead fish; it caresses the body with a warm palm or slaps needles of cold into unprotected cheeks. Lesser winds than the castaways' nor'wester have overturned small craft, and people have died in the river's sullen, wind-created chop.

But step back a hundred feet, go farther inland past the hedgerows, and wind's force is blunted. Along the dirt road and in the back fields, the air may even seem completely motionless except for the faint vertical currents on which smoke rises or spiderlings balloon straight up, up, up on their silken parachutes. Over the water, wind takes apparent respite only on the dog days of deepest summer and during the calms, brief as hyphens, in which it seems to hold its breath while switching from an offshore to an onshore mode or back again. Otherwise, the wind on the river is always active, always restless.

"Always alive," I would say if I were a Greek in Homer's day. Sons of Astraios and Eos—the Glittering Stars and the Dawn—the winds were born wholly exempt from time and death. They are four brothers, and each has his name and personality. Notos, the rain-bringer, sweeps up from the south. Euros flows fair out of the east. Zephyros, friend from the gentle west, is husband to every green-growing thing. Boreas spreads icy white wings and screams like an eagle out of the north. And if I were that long-ago Greek, I would know that winds affect fertility as well as cause harsh or pleasant weather. Sometimes, their breath congeals or kills; then chickens and ducks and mourning doves lay wind-eggs that will never hatch. More often, the brothers act as forces for increase. Homer states quite plainly in the *Iliad* that Boreas turned himself into a black-maned stallion for love of twelve mares, and he covered each of them; later, twelve colts raced over fields of grain without breaking one single seed head from its stalk, and they skimmed over the sea with hooves barely touching the whitecapped waves. I would know, too, that children are blown into their mothers' wombs by wind.

In another place, in a time immeasurably more ancient that Homer's, the soul in the wind made primal exhalation. In the beginning, says the King James version of Genesis, "The Spirit of God moved over the face of the waters." The New English Bible translates the same passage as "a mighty wind swept over the surface of the waters." Something is missing, however, in both of these versions. In the first rendering, the words lie like a ship in irons: Where is the wind? In the second, the wind blows but is hollow, empty of divine intent. And in both, the sound of what is happening is muffled or lost. But the people whose story this is, who told it out loud year after year through countless generations, knew the sound. And the scribe who finally put the story in writing preserved the exact word. Hebrew has it right: *ruach*—rush-of-spirit. And when that word is given breath—*roooo-aaaaah*—we can still hear the sound of the ancient event, the soughing and roaring. But it's not the wind's voice that we hear. It's the maelstrom's awed response at being quickened by that timeless breath.

Christina Rossetti might have asked, "Who has heard the wind?" and replied as she did to the question about seeing it. The wind has no voice of its own. Instead, it is a musician fingering the nearest instrument. Dry leaves clatter, electric wires produce a vibrant hum, water slap-crashes on the bulkhead, and stays clank-clank against the slender masts of Flying Scots. *Rooooo-aaaaah*, daily we hear the ancient song that primeval water sang when rush-of-spirit touched its face.

The lesser winds of Great Neck Point do not impregnate mares or women, and only at a great and muted distance do they echo creation's stupendous roar. But when a zephyr breezes lightly in, imagination flowers; when northerlies strike with whetted talons, imagination rides their eagle wings and hears the screaming whistle of gale winds moving through the feathers. Listening to wind music is like listening to a chanting, singing language that hypnotizes even though it cannot be understood. It seems possible that the human singers of narratives—the Genesis poet, Homer, Virgil, and all their named and nameless descendants—have taken lessons from the wind and used its tricks to give their story-songs compelling voice—changes of pace and volume, pauses for suspense and catching breath, onomatopoeia, repetition, riddles. Like the wind, the best singers need not refer to any text; they know their tales by heart. The Greek word for poet, *poietes*, means maker, creator. At

Great Neck Point, it often seems that there never is a world for us except the one wind orchestrates and, in its orchestration, makes.

How lacking in music, the scientific explanations for divine breath, for Boreas and his more moderate brothers: that air moves, stirs itself to breeze or hurricane, expands and contracts in response to temperature differentials and to the heating and cooling of earth's surfaces, be they solid or fluid. When land is warm, the air above it heats and rises, leaving a space for cooler air to move in off the water. The effect takes place in reverse when water is warmer than land. This general theme plays out in countless, sometimes contrapuntal variations. In one common event, the air chases its tail: We watch as low clouds, galloping southward, skim the far shore like swift, grey colts; far above them, larger clouds tower and billow, rolling sun-shot to the north. And the river acts as a great funnel, channeling wind upstream or down between its banks.

Here and on any body of water, the wind makes necessary music. When water is its instrument, waves rise, curl over on themselves, crash, and lapse in a spumy white hiss. A friend, a trained scientist who airily calls himself a "bubble-ologist," explains the import of the water's song. Although bubble-chasing sounds frothy, it is serious work. "It has to do," he says, "with basic research into how water receives and retains oxygen."

But water is H_2O. It comprises two atoms of hydrogen bonded to one of oxygen, and isn't oxygen the breath of life?

Of course, he says, but nothing alive is able to breathe pure water. From fish to barnacles, crabs to jellyfish and sandworms, every marine and freshwater creature depends on dissolved atmospheric oxygen. Wind, like the stiff westerly churning the river as he talks, acts as an aerator, charging the water with oxygen that's breathable. Cool temperatures are the cap that keeps the fizz in the liquid. Without dissolved oxygen, the water's children drown. They are suffocated just as surely as the human being who draws water into his lungs. At least once each summer, sometimes more often, we see the flounder casting themselves ashore and the blue crabs clambering up the seawalls in a desperate quest for breathable air. Long ago, the Roman naturalist Pliny noticed the same phenomenon on Mediterranean shores—fish panting in the summer heat and gasping during spells of calm. The dissolved oxygen in their watery demesne is gone, sucked up by weeks on end of almost windless heat.

Such leaching, though, is not the only reason that the river's liquid air may be diminished. Another is that algae, nourished by runoff fertilizer or industrial wastes, may bloom prodigious and then decay. The rotting of this vegetable matter steals oxygen with a furtive efficiency equal to that of still air and heat. And heat, bringing the algae soup to a slow simmer, may exacerbate the problem. Wind is part of the cure.

A breath of fresh air, a good stiff breeze, and bubble-whitened waves—that's what we need. Not just flounder and crabs, but all of us—people, dogs, eagles, and maybe even mosquitoes—can do with such bracing.

The camper-castaways carousing in our yard are thoroughly braced. Ostensibly, they wait for the wind to become more amicable. And the waiting is lively, with two dozen perpetual-motion machines tumbling over the grass and shouting. The young'uns seem not to care if they ever return to camp and their suppers. I'm told that they were scared when they first reached our solid shore. But not anymore; the accident of arrival has become the occasion for a holiday. A muscular counselor helps us pull our hundred-yard gill net ashore, and we hold an ad hoc class in identifying marine species—bluefish, croaker, silver butterfish with bellies dipped in gold, one newly molted crab as soft and limp as a jellyfish. The Chief brings out celebratory cans of soda. These Tweakers, as their age group is called at camp, have been well trained: Empty cans are not pitched into the river nor tossed at random on the grass but stowed tidily in our recycling bin.

Inside the trailer, I ask the counselor-in-charge, the one who's smoking, why Flying Scots were launched in a wind like this.

He shrugs. "We followed the plan for the day. The plan just didn't follow us."

"There must have been small-craft warnings. She was blowing up a
gale this morning when I left for town."

"Nope. They don't do warnings here unless we're looking at a hurricane."

He's right and he's wrong. Warnings are issued—a line that flashes
bright green for five seconds on the TV forecaster's chart of current conditions, a two-second radio squib amid rock music or droning reports on
the price of hogs. In their brevity, these warnings can slip by unnoticed.
Detailed weather reports are continuously available, of course, through
the broadcasts of NOAA, the National Oceanic and Atmospheric Ad-
ministration—if one has the small radio receiver needed (and if its bat-
teries have juice). Most river-dwellers, however, rely mainly on long
acquaintance with the river; they check the colors of the water and sniff
the air. For the direction of the wind and a guess at its speed, the Chief
and I check the wind sock atop a metal pole erected on the riverbank
near the fish-cleaning table. The sock comes in various guises—a black-
and-white loon with long tail-feather streamers; a rainbow-striped carp;
or, currently, a Don't-Tread-on-Me flag, the South Carolina Gadsden
Regiment version of 1776, with its rattlesnake coiled on a bright yellow
ground. Right now, that flag is stretched full out, snapping in the wind.
Seems to us that anyone along this shore, anyone with a lick of good
sense, could have read treachery in today's weather.

I try again. "Good thing you found a safe port. But what possessed you
to hoist sail in wind like this?"

"The challenge," he says, "the adventure." And he tells us a tale of setting out last year with a bunch of apprentice seamen in sixteen-foot cata-
marans. They were bound across Pamlico Sound for the Outer Banks and

a night of camping. When fair weather turned suddenly foul, high winds and breaking seas appearing out of nowhere to disable several boats, rescue was effected by the Coast Guard. The Chief and I shake our heads. He is young, in his tenderest twenties, and therefore still immortal.

The wind of castaways does not abate. This time exercising commendable leadership, counselor-in-charge telephones the camp. Not long afterward, a chase boat with an outboard motor and a stable tri-hull design roars up to our pier and off-loads a gang of experienced hands, enough to sail the fleet of Flying Scots back to home port. An hour and a half later, after having lost its way twice on sidewinding rural roads, the camp's bus pulls into the yard, and the campers scramble aboard. The bus departs with song issuing lustily through its open windows: "Ninety-nine bottles of beer on the wall, ninety-nine bottles of beer . . . ."

We learn what an adventure the kids had when counselor-in-charge calls to thank us and to tell us that this batch of Tweakers has chosen as its special sobriquet "The Chiefs of Great Neck Point." He asks if we might allow groups of older campers and counselors-in-training to make planned overnight stays in our yard. Of course. All we need is a little advance notice.

Later this summer, and in summers to follow, they will arrive. They'll pull their boats ashore, erect their brown bubble-tents on the grass, feed us camp-style on spaghetti and canned fruit cocktail fancified with marshmallows, and invite us to join the campfire circle just before bedtime. In the morning, they'll breakfast, pack their gear, and sail away, leaving no evidence that the yard has been occupied for sixteen hours by a rollicking navy. Only once will we find a left-behind item—a pair of dainty pink bikini underpants. The Chief will give them the only possible treatment—he'll lower the rattlesnake from the wind-sock pole and raise the pink pants.

But future campers won't always give prior notice. Sometimes the only warning will come on the wind. When the breeze hauls— BOOM!—and the weather turns surly, we'll look for sails. Want to or not, Flying Scots or Zumas or little Sunfish will fetch up on our shore, some come sailing bravely all the way, others dismasted and towed in by the chase boat. The campers will disembark, pull their puny craft ashore, and huddle shivering, teeth a-chatter, in the cold, pelting embrace of wind-blown rain.

Though we're twentieth-century cognizant of the physical circumstances causing unseen, unheard atmospheric gases to move hither and yon, the Chief and I prefer the Homeric view, that the wind is alive. And, though many of our neighbors at the Point wouldn't be so crazy as to say so out loud, they'd nod their heads in agreement. Granted, wind is unpredictable, unreasoning, passionless, immane. It creates, giving air to marine life and bringing us nurture. It destroys, unmaking our most careful maps and taking all too many shipwrecked sacrifices on the river's altar. Better that we treat it as an eagle, a stallion, or a jealous spouse. It blew with spirit at earth's beginning, will blow at earth's end and through all the turning days between. Better still that we honor it as the breath of something perduring, something (for all we know) divine.

up the

creek

b ut I do have a paddle. That's all to
the good for someone who hadn't expected to be traveling up this creek
or any other, and certainly not on the steamiest afternoon yet of a hot
and dripping summer.

All day, the far shore of the wide and salty Neuse has been obscured
behind a thick scrim of haze. The river itself seems motionless, stretch-

ing between its banks like a great, glaring slick of light. The sky overhead
is as pale as a bone. It's ninety-six degrees, the air wringing wet and the
heat index somewhere in the hellish range. Till our nineteen-year-old
neighbor K. D. came on the scene, I'd managed most successfully to stay
indoors, hiding in the cool, dry hum of the air conditioner. I wrote letters, picked a pound of crabmeat, and discovered at last the source of the
scritch-scratching heard recently in the small, dark hours—a mouse nest
under construction.

K. D. ambled in to visit midway through the crabs. In two more
weeks, she will march off to Navy boot camp, but right now she suffers
from as bad a case of the fidgets as a child waiting for Christmas. To
while away the next few hours, and bring the Navy that much closer,
she'd planned to go messing about in a boat—a canoe, to be exact, borrowed from her cousin. Would I like to come along up the creek?

There was nothing on my agenda between crabs and supper. Why
not?

"Good," said our local version of the Water Rat. "I hoped you would."

So here we are at 3:00 P.M., the Rat and an ad hoc Mole, paddling upriver toward the mouth of the creek. The canoe is a well-weathered alu-
minum model, fifteen feet long and beamy, with a squared-off stern.
Sometimes K. D.'s three-years-younger cousin attaches a two-horse
trolling motor and goes angling for bluefish out in the river or sunfish up
in the pond, but this afternoon we travel on muscle power. In no time,
sweat oils our arms and faces and drenches our shirts. We're not working
hard, though. The current offers no resistance, nor is there any wind to
push against. The only breeze is the one we create, air slipping gently,
deliciously over our skins as we glide forward.

Dip and sweep, lift and feather. Water beads on the edge of my paddle; the droplets fall and rest for a moment on the silvery surface of the
river before they are resorbed. It takes five minutes, no more, to paddle
from K. D.'s pier to the creek mouth. Turning, the sun now beating on
our backs, we head into the creek.

Called Courts on the nautical chart and Coaches in come-lately local parlance, the creek meanders into the river from the east. A stretch of sand, partly overgrown with beargrass yuccas, wistaria, and toadflax, lies just downriver of its mouth; the upriver side is marked by a tiny island of spartina grass, a favorite hangout for the great blue herons. Here they often stand in long-legged elegance, not moving but poised for an instant lunge at any passing minnows or crabs.

Something waits like a heron at the edge of this afternoon's brilliant, sultry calm. Be it a big splash or maybe just the merest ripple, something is going to happen. It's that kind of day. But right now we paddle, and K. D. talks about the Navy.

The creek mouth is as straight and narrow as the tube of a funnel. It reaches inland for about one hundred yards before it opens into twenty acres of brackish pond. In this short stretch, I've seen raccoons paddling across in every season; young mud snakes, patterned black and rosy orange, swimming in early summer through the needlerushes at water's edge; big golden carp tumbling in the springtime shallows as they mate; and, twice, a lone, wintering snipe resting on a low-water mudflat. A notable sight: In these parts, the common snipe is a skittish, reclusive bird, not common at all. But today, apart from the hovering and darting of big, blue-headed dragonflies, nothing special catches my eye.

Dip and sweep—no, dip and shove. We use the paddles to push ourselves over the sandbar that guards the entrance to the Courts Creek pond. Usually, the surface of the pond is ruffled by some breath of air, but today it lies flat and smooth as silvered glass.

Two inches of water cover the sandbar. When dry weather or a steady southwest wind lowers the water level, the bar lies exposed and almost blocks the entrance to the pond. Standing on the creek bank then with binoculars and spotting scope, I scan it for plovers and sandpipers and the tricolored herons that frequent the coast but only occasionally appear this far upriver. This afternoon, the usual birds are here—red-winged blackbirds clinging to slender stems, green-backed herons hunched on low snags to watch the water, and one great egret wading up to its backwards knees, which are really its heels, beside the green-gray rushes.

We paddle across the pond, making for its southeastern corner and the upper reaches of the creek. K. D. talks of her hopes to enter hospital corpsman school right after boot camp. I listen with half an ear.

The pond provides shelter, food, and recreation for many creatures. Muskrat, beaver, river otter—all of these use it as a playground and a thoroughfare. Marsh ducks dabble in the waterweeds at its inland end. Fiddler crabs burrow in the sodden clay around the cordgrass roots. Snakes—not just mud snakes but corn snakes, rat snakes, cottonmouths, three or four varieties of water snake—breed in its environs and dine heartily on frogs, turtles, and fish. People are also summoned to the pond by the abounding fish—feisty largemouth bass and plump, succulent sunfish, the redbreasts and pumpkinseeds, which everyone here calls robins. And I've seen people, who didn't see me, boat into the pond for another reason: It seems an ideally private place for sunbathing in the buff. But nobody else is here today, not fishermen with clothes on nor sun worshipers without a stitch. And, apart from our paddles and the canoe's puny wake, nothing disturbs the pond's surface except the hook-billed snouts of snapping turtles.

Anything might lurk beneath this placid water, this mirror that reflects everything above its upper, silver side but hides everything that lies below.

"Look there," K. D. says. "I have *got* to check that out."

Midway across the pond, a buoy rests on the water. Weathered and dingy, it looks more like a clump of pondweed than a man-made marker. I wouldn't have seen it without K. D.—nor have been on the pond in the first place waiting for something to happen.

Shipping her paddle, she leans over the side. I lean quickly in the opposite direction lest the canoe turn turtle and dump both of us overboard. Better by far to stay afloat. Though the pond is shallow, I know from incautious, years-ago experience that the mud on its bottom is ankle- to knee-deep and nowhere affords reliable footing. K. D. grabs the Styrofoam buoy and pulls on a frayed black line that's gummy with dead algae. And hauls up a crab pot. It contains one listless jimmy crab. Lord knows how long he's lingered in captivity. She lets him go but brings the pot on board for taking home. Finders, keepers—aside from which, setting crab pots in the pond violates the fish and wildlife regulations. She wipes mucky hands on her jeans and picks up the paddle.

A fish leaps from the silver water into the light. A moment ago, nothing was here. Now there is. And suddenly—plip!—isn't. Almost at once, the ripples subside. Wrapped in shimmering, trembly heat, what is real is not, and what is not real is. Everything can change in a single instant.

An escort of osprey—two of them, three, five—gathers overhead, calling the stroke with their loud, sweet cries. Dip, sweep, lift, feather, we round the bend into the upper creek. And there are more buoys. One pair close at hand, a second pair yonder, linked by a line of corks, they mark a gill net. The season for using gill nets in inland waters such as these runs from early December until June. The corkline on this one looks filthy. Someone must have set and abandoned it last spring.

"Gross," K. D. says. "Can't take it with us, but we can sure fish it on the way back out."

Anything may be tangled in its careless meshes—mullet, bass, red drum, blue crabs, snapping turtles, a duck that dabbled too far and too deep for safety. Or the net may have caught something less ordinary, such as an alligator. Once abundant on this coast, now listed as endangered, alligators—and a growing population of them, too—are certainly living in local streams and marshes. But only unsupported rumor has placed them recently in Courts Creek. The paths trampled through rushes and cordgrass, the slides in the mud, are the work of otters. Otter, alligator—no, we shall not find such muscular animals trapped in flimsy monofilament.

But a naiad—now there's a possibility. Every river and lake, every spring and fountain in classical Greece had its resident naiad, its very own indwelling spirit. One could catch glimpses of her in the water's gleam and sparkle, could hear her in its rush and gurgle. Why should there not be such spirits in the New World? And why not a particular naiad who fancies brackish water and makes her home within Courts Creek? Her domain would include not only the fish and the otters, the crabs and the pond grasses but her namesakes as well. Science has borrowed her excellent name to designate the aquatic larvae of aerial creatures such as mayflies, damselflies, and the dragonflies that hover and dart not only in the creek mouth but here in its slowly narrowing upper reaches.

"By the rushes, what's that?" K. D. says abruptly.

We've startled a mallard. Standing on a mudflat at water's edge, it was preening. Now it slips behind the rushes and out of our sight. A drake in drab summer dress or a hen in the usual modest brown? I don't know. We paddle on. The wheeling, calling escort of osprey has increased to six. I can count the real birds overhead or their reflections on the silver water.

Or an undine—there might be an undine in the net, not tangled and trapped but simply resting there as if it were a hammock. According to the scientist who provided the first definitive description of her kind, she is the elemental, the supernatural principle without which water cannot exist. And the name he gave her, Undina, means She-Who-Is-Made-of-Waves, although the situation is precisely the other way around—the waves are made entirely of her. Nor is she alone; she shares the power to form and animate the world with three cohorts. Her sovereign domain is water, and they rule the other three classical elements: The gnome molds earth and dwells within it; the salamander defines and inhabits fire; the sylph—mortal, unlike the other three, but lacking a soul—gives air its inspiration and its liveliness.

The scientist who investigated these matters was something of a strange fish in his own right. A Swiss-born physician and alchemist who practiced in the early decades of the sixteenth century, he was the first to prepare the pain-killing tincture of opium known as laudanum, which he gussied up with other ingredients such as gold and pearls. He also gussied himself up with a truly resplendent name—Philippus Aureolus Paracelsus, or Philip the Golden Better-than-Celsus. (Celsus, under the Roman emperor Tiberius early in the first century A.D., wrote an encyclopedic treatise on medicine that languished for a millennium, then gained admiration and many readers in the Middle Ages.) But who can fault Paracelsus, born von Hohenheim, for choosing such a gleaming pseudonym when the name his parents had wished upon him was Theophrastus Bombastus?

If an undine is not to be found in the net, I may at least find pleasure in contemplating a Paracelsian tenet with a fine contemporary resonance: The life of humankind is part and parcel, indivisibly, of all that the universe contains. Dip and sweep.

We're well up the creek now. And it's ten calling osprey that wheel overhead, ten mirror images that fly beneath our hull. Suddenly, small birds hidden till now make loud and visible advertisements. Common yellowthroats—males wearing black domino masks—cling to the cordgrass and belt out their cheerful *wee-weechy* song. Chickadees chatter, gnatcatchers lisp and buzz, a white-eyed vireo clicks on, sings its tune, clicks off.

K. D. stops paddling. "I wonder," she says, "how often they'll let us call home from boot camp."

In her nineteen years, apart from overnights with friends and a single week at 4-H camp, she's spent almost no time away from home and family. In two more weeks, she'll be off on her own.

"Often enough," I tell her. "Now paddle, unless you want me to push us in circles. I'm highly skilled at boating in circles."

"Yeah," says the Water Rat, "I've seen you row."

Before she puts the canoe into forward motion, I dip a hand in the water, then lick my fingers. Mmm, salty. And on we go. As we round the next bend, a wood duck skitters off the water and disappears into creekside vegetation. Along this stretch, needle rushes share the marshy banks with seashore mallows. In this last week of July, the mallows have unfolded into full bloom, showing thousands on thousands of small, pink, roselike flowers.

The creek narrows—two canoe lengths wide, then one—and the air is as thick and steamy as that in a sauna. The woodland of baldcypress and loblolly pines presses closer to the banks. Among them stand a few dead trees, their gaunt trunks weathered to a luminous grey. Some of the tallest of these snags are crowned with osprey nests, a fact that explains our escort, now a dozen strong and increasingly shrill. Other snags have toppled, and a few of these deadfalls now lie halfway across the creek like vine-covered bridges that no one got around to finishing. Some we can paddle around; others we must duck. I look for snakes, which often lie motionless on branches that overhang the water.

What if the abandoned gill net holds something less pleasant than a naiad or an undine? The grassy pond-bottom meadows on which the marsh ducks feed might also offer pasturage to a New World subspecies of Scotland's loch-dwelling kelpie, which is a water spirit variously formed in the shape of a colt or a heifer. Kelpies are as frisky as the creatures they resemble but not so innocent, for their favorite sport is to drown unwary travelers.

The pond might shelter other beings that are equally dangerous but much less ordinary in appearance. The nix that lurks in Germanic folklore might also lurk here. Half woman, half fish, she croons a song that entices human company to her fine underwater palace. The poet Walter de la Mare, who heard and obviously resisted the fatal singing, described the nix's voice as "haunting, penetrating, pining." Or the net may have caught her male counterpart, the nikker. He is a monster, evil incarnate, like the Anglo-Saxon Grendel, who crawled from a lake and sated his appetite with men. But we won't find Grendel himself in the net, nor his mother who lived in the lake's ooze, for the hero Beowulf did them in long ago. Nonetheless, it may be that Courts Creek pond should be posted with warnings.

Whirrrr! Something rises. Monster? No, bird, and a small one at that.

As it zips out of sight, I see just enough—barred tail, solid brown wings—to know that it's not just another of the spotted sandpipers that are common by the river in the summertime. This one—it must have been feeding along the bank—is a solitary sandpiper, the first I've seen in five years.

Could be there's something better in the net than monsters, something as soft and appealing as a duckling. A water-baby? It was the English clergyman Charles Kingsley, at one point chaplain to Queen Victoria, who first catalogued that kind of sprite in his 1863 book *The Water-Babies*. There he fully describes their habits and habitats by chronicling the adventures of young Tom the chimney sweep, who never once washed himself until, by a fortunate mischance, he becomes unexpectedly eligible for metamorphosis.

In a twist on the water-to-air transformation of the dragonfly's naiad, Tom's change takes him from land into water. And there, completely bereft of all clothing and grime, he discovers with gleeful surprise "how comfortable it [is] to have nothing on himself but himself." Much else, however, is not a bit comfortable. Newly amphibious, wearing a mudpuppy's collar of feathery gills, Tom must acquire the good manners to which he was never made privy in all his terrestrial days. Not only must he learn to live harmoniously with other water-babies, but he must attend most carefully to the lessons taught by two hardworking, ever-vigilant old ladies, Mrs. Bedonebyasyoudid and her gentler sister Mrs. Doasyouwouldbedoneby.

Throughout this definitive treatise on water-babies, the Rev. Mr. Kingsley gives frequent and trenchant commentaries on their domain. People have always noticed the health or degradation of their waters, though they haven't always made much fuss about what they've seen. But from the upper reaches of the twentieth century, Mr. Kingsley's nineteenth-century concern for water quality seems almost prescient. Tom's first lesson is taught by a river while he's still on land. As it flows chiming and tinkling through the countryside, the river sings:

Clear and cool, clear and cool,
By laughing shallow and dreaming pool . . .
Undefiled, for the undefiled;
Play by me, bathe in me, mother and child.

But as the river winds closer to the shore, its song changes:

Dank and foul, dank and foul,
By the smoky town in its murky cowl . . .
Who dare sport with the sin-defiled?
Shrink from me, turn from me, mother and child.

Farther down, when small Tom's river enters the sea, once again it flows free and clean, "Like a soul that has sinned and is pardoned again." But not every river can sing such a song.

The Neuse might. Or, if it hasn't sung loudly or much in recent times, it may do so soon. These days, volunteers test the waters every week. On our stretch of riverbank, rain or shine, howling nor'easter or sweaty stillness like today's, K. D.'s grandfather monitors the river's health, taking its temperature, measuring salinity and dissolved oxygen, and—oh my!

"Beg pardon?" K. D. says.

"I said, 'Mr. Doasyouwouldbedoneby.' "

"Run that by me one more time."

"Mr. Doasyouwouldbedoneby. Little brother of a lady with the same name." And I tell her a little of young Tom's story.

"Kid should've run away and joined the Navy. What should I go for, one hitch or two?"

"You're the only one can figure that out."

We fall into companionable silence, dip and sweep. This far up, the pines and cypresses grow closer to the banks. The creek is narrowing rapidly, its water reflecting the golden green of bankside grasses and mallow leaves. Soon, a deadfall spanning its entire width will block our way, or else we'll be so pinched between the banks that we'll have to back out. But at this point we can still maneuver around a jutting snag, weathered almost white and embellished, if that's the word, with—

"Ohh," K. D. whispers on indrawn breath. "Ohh."

Whiskers, bright eyes, an otter. Two otters. No farther than a paddle's length away.

Up, down, up—pop go the otters. Up, they cock their glistening heads and eye us with the utmost curiosity. We're given five full inspections. Down, they set the surface aswirl with the vigor of their underwater acrobatics. Then, as suddenly as they appeared, they're gone. The water, no longer rumpled, regains its glassy finish.

"Ohh." K. D. has never before been so close to river otters. I have, but only as they've swum past my home, along the seawall or under the pier. But now I'm floating around in *their* home.

"They must sun here," she says, indicating the loose, black embellishment on the bleached-white snag.

"Raccoon scat. Look at the seeds. If it were otters, you'd just see fish bones. Aside from which, otters are more fastidious than 'coons—that's what your granddad tells me. They use a particular place rather than just letting loose wherever they're at."

We back up a little, turn, and head down the creek at a slow but steady pace. K. D. does not say another word about the Navy. She doesn't say anything at all. The osprey still cry above, still wheel in the mirror around our hull, but fall away as we travel toward the pond. And no snakes bask on today's branches or wriggle through the water. Dip and sweep, lift and feather, it is as if we move down a long, loose sleeve of stillness, heat, and brilliant light. And I think as we paddle along that the presence of otters augurs well for the creek.

As a body of water worth cherishing, the wide and salty Neuse has recently garnered much public attention. K. D.'s grandfather and the faithful others who test its waters every week have been in the vanguard of its caretakers. And this year a riverkeeper, brought on stream by a private foundation, acts as the first-ever overall guardian for our thirty-mile stretch of rolling, grey-brown water. Spreading his efforts into the tributaries, he has recruited a platoon of creekkeepers, who look for algae blooms and unwonted fish-kills. Most of the kept creeks, however, are those that have attracted people, who have constructed piers and marinas, set up fish camps and mobile-home parks, and sometimes built elegant houses along the creek banks. A few such dwellings stand along the riverfront just upstream of Courts Creek. Because peddling real estate brings in far more profits than growing trees, a major timber company has developed the land upriver of the creek into lots of several acres each.

Soon, there will be houses on the pondfront, too. None have sprouted yet, but someone has already signaled his intentions by constructing a wooden walkway that connects higher ground with the pond. It bridges a small marsh and ends in a platform over the water. In the owner's customary absence, local people go there to cast a line and reel in dinner.

But Courts Creek is wild in its upper reaches and may stay that way for two or three human lifetimes—that is, till entropy declares that everything be silted up. For generations the creek has welled from a great sponge of water-saturated earth, and its course to the pond winds through several square miles of wetlands—not the debatable come-and-go kind, but wetlands in a constant state of ooze and trickle. No permits are issued for building houses and docks in such soggy places. The only man-made constructions allowed are blinds and tree stands for hunters and nest boxes for wood ducks.

Otters are the keepers of Courts Creek. And as long as they stay loyal to the job, their presence will bear witness to the good health of water and habitat.

"Coming up on the net," K. D. says. "Wonder what's in it."

My heart gives a leap. Anything! Turtle, fish, naiad, undine, what shall it be? Not a water-baby, please. But maybe old Theophrastus Bombastus his very self!

"No, stay where you are. I'll manage," says Ratty to her passenger, the Mole. She pulls up the marker buoys on one end. "God, this thing is heavy."

The reason for the net's considerable weight is that the netting itself is ancient, a rotting, algae-gummed remnant of a day long gone. It's made of cotton, and the cotton has soaked up gallons of water. These days, no one takes the time and care to hand-tie such gill nets, especially not when strong and inexpensive nylon monofilament is available. That lightweight, waterproof fabric can be attached to cork and lead lines in a matter of hours. This net, however, has not been lingering in the pond since cotton went out of style. The buoys are new, and one is marked with the name and address of a well-known local scofflaw. Likely, he used this antiquated net, which was just lying around, to save himself the expense of buying a new one.

There are no creatures in the net at all, not one. And the cotton bunting has been so weakened by age and immersion that almost anything caught could break free. Nonetheless, K. D. says that she'll pick it up before she departs for boot camp.

Dip, sweep, lift, feather. In silence, we cross the pond, its water no longer silver but gilded by the westering sun. A shove over the sandbar and, a minute later, we slide into the river for the last lap home. Our paddles plunge, the river laps softly at its shore, and the laughing gulls jeer as they always do.

K. D. speaks up when we reach her pier and disembark. "Glad you could come along. I really needed some ballast in the bow."

She's a rat, all right, the kind that doesn't deserve a capital letter. But then she says, "Write to me sometimes, okay?"

Okay. Bemused and happy, I walk on home. It hasn't cooled off one whit. And what, exactly, *has* happened on this still, bright, dripping-hot afternoon?

the mad swimmer
of beeman cove

Where is the language to describe these odd little islands? Where are the metaphors to ease them into some semblance of familiarity, to set them in a context that I can understand? It's a formality, nothing more, to say that they belong to New Zealand. The truth is, they belong only to themselves. And their situation in the subantarctic makes them almost as unapproachable as the stars.

Nonetheless, I'm here. Dislodged from ordinary time and space, I find myself amid a most peculiar concatenation of things and events, as if I'd been given a ringside seat at a cosmic variety show.

This happens: On a sandy shore, a roly-poly champagne blonde rears up, lunges, and roars, showing sharp white teeth. I hurry past. Lunge, roar, brandish teeth—the next *jolie* blonde along my route and the next and the one after repeat the performance. I'm sure it's clear to these animals that I am not one of their kind, not a Hooker's sea lion cow. It's not at all clear what I am, but that doesn't matter. And so, the focus of a great, lurching, noisy, inquisitive hullabaloo, I move right smartly down the beach to the path leading inland. What is this commotion all about? I learn that, in body language as stylized and exact as movements in classical ballet, the animals were simply inviting me to play.

This happens: A hundred yards inland, fat sea lion pups, five and six weeks old, snooze in gold-red-brown communal heaps. One wakes, wriggles out from under, and belly-scoots with great speed toward a small stream. There it stops to bleat—*maa-aa-aa-aa*—in a voice as tremulous and heartbroken as that of a lamb calling for its mother. Another pup abandons its dreams to investigate my boots. When they prove uninteresting, it finds my life jacket lying on the ground, picks up a strap in its small sharp teeth, and gives a tentative tug. The whole blaze-orange contraption slides forward. Pup tugs again. Tug and slide—a new game! When I put out a hand to retrieve the jacket, I touch the unwitting thief. How thick and coarse the rust-colored fur. Giving a shudder, the little animal looks up with utter surprise: How dare you! Or, more likely perhaps, I didn't know you were alive.

This happens: Later, on a mountain height, I round a tussock of snow grass and come nose to bill with a royal albatross atop its nest. In flight, with its dark, slender wings extended to a span of nearly twelve feet, the bird sailplanes on demonic winds with the grace of an angel. Now, the great wings are folded and tucked against the gleaming body. Tending to most important work, the bird sits on its egg unperturbed by the sudden apparition of another species. It does, however, acknowledge my presence. It points its long, pale bill at the sky and almost inaudibly clacks its mandibles.

And if the animals are unafraid, the flora are quite immodest. The flowering plants called megaherbs—"giant greenery"—put out leaves the size of platters to catch every morsel of sunlight during the here-and-gone subantarctic summer. The forests, the world's most southerly, grow as gnarled and grasping as any woods conjured by fearful imagination. The trees, known by their Maori name of *rata*, stand densely packed, their twisted black trunks trimmed with frills of ghostly grey lichen. But the darkness of these forests gives shelter not to witches but to penguins and pigs and rabbits with fur the color of tarnished silver.

Here all the animals, including me, can walk on water. Almost everywhere, even on mountain ridges, bedrock is overlaid with peat that is five, eight, eleven meters deep. And peat is fibrous stuff with an unquenchable thirst, sopping up the torrential subantarctic rains, which it holds like a great sponge. The burden of water is slowly released in seepage and trickles that gather and swell into swift little streams, which in turn find their way to the sea as narrow cataracts plunging off cliffs or blowing like silver ribbons on the wind. Of course, I'm not the only person on this oozy scene. Water wells up in the tracks of some twenty-odd others, who also traipse through the dank, enchanted forests and march—their steps far more sprightly than mine—up and up over saturated soil to the albatross heights.

Two of this company are not satisfied merely to be atop the water but must be in it. In the company of penguins and sea lions, they slide into the salt waves of an open bay or the calm of a sheltered cove. Often, the most that can be seen of the Malacologist is the tip of her snorkel or a splashing flipper. She's collecting shellfish. Young Garry, clad in briefs of royal-blue nylon, simply goes swimming. Total immersion, then a vigorous crawl or breaststroke, and he rises, beaming, to wade ashore with the uplifted arms of a winner. Blue is certainly his color. Onshore he carries a small royal-blue umbrella. He may be a Munchkin, one of those blue-loving people freed by Dorothy from the Wicked Witch of the East.

The Land of Oz—that's the first metaphor to offer itself, and I grab. I've known about Oz all my life, knew about it even before Judy Garland sang and danced Hollywood's version of the place into cinematic immortality. And here I am, whirled away and set down in a magical kingdom.

It may as well be Oz. The comparison is hardly far-fetched. It's not just the latter-day Munchkin, not just the wealth of wonders and improbabilities that qualify these odd little places, these specks of wave- and storm-battered land, for legendary status. Like Oz, they exist on a plane well-nigh invisible to the cartographers. Only the largest-scale maps give token recognition to their presence in the vast and chilly sea—mere dots that indicate land, names in tiny print. But from November through February—the upside-down austral summer, when daylight banishes most of the night—these two-bit islands shine as green and brave as the Emerald City.

They are, however, slightly more accessible than Oz. For hundreds of miles, the yellow brick road traverses the Southern Ocean down and down through the wind-blasted latitudes known as the roaring forties and the furious fifties. The mode of transport is not, of course, a tornado but a very small ship that climbs the crests, crashes down in the troughs of twelve-meter swells. Though Toto is forbidden and none of my companions is fashioned of straw, tin, or cowardice, a few are certainly gadabouts, collecting exotic destinations—Kilimanjaro, Punta Arenas, these tiny subantarctic islands set like chips of emerald in the great grey sea— in the same way that other pack-rat types collect matchbooks or souvenir spoons. Young Garry has put visits to forty-five countries in his trophy book; this time he stays within the limits of his native land, though he says he's thinking seriously of emigrating to Australia. Others travel the sea road to observe birds or photograph wildlife and land-scapes. Several are botanists, island-hopping to study what one of them calls the "life-styles" of plants that are so little known that many lack common names. I have joined this motley company at the invitation of not the Wizard, exactly, but our expedition leader—call him the Guide—who speaks with soft but messianic fervor about the "spiritual dimension" of our journey.

And now that I'm well and truly embarked on adventure, alternately rolling and pitching with the ocean-driven movements of a very small ship or scrambling slowly over precipitous peat bogs and meeting animals untutored in fear, I find that it's up to me to figure out what I'm doing in such strange places. Not only are they almost impossibly remote from other bodies of land, but they are foreign to all my experience and comprehension. Oz? My imagination understands that magical land far better then this one. Oz won't quite do. There's need to hunt for other metaphoric handles on the situation.

Neither the Malacologist nor young Garry has any doubts whatsoever about why they're here and what they're doing. Both are happy as ducks in the rain or frogs in a big new puddle.

The Malacologist, hovering at the half-century mark, is weathered and ebullient. Crow's-feet radiate from the corner of her blue eyes, and lines are carved deep around her excellent smile. She smiles often and broadly, a woman in love. And the objects of her passion are almost all she talks about. Limpets, snails, sea slugs, mollusks with shells, mollusks without—or possibilities for finding such because nobody knows what's really here—have lured her down over the swelling, tumultuous waves to Ocean Beach and Sandy Bay, Camp Cove and Perseverance Harbor. Love took her by surprise several years ago when, with nothing better to do, she decided to look into the activities of a club devoted to studying mollusks. Now, to her delight and great astonishment, she's a bootstrap marine scientist, an amateur in the truest sense: someone without formal training who pursues a discipline not for money but for love of its specific complexities. Now, while terrestrial and aerial phenomena fascinate the rest of us, she tugs on a wet suit and slips into the briny like a seal—except that a seal wouldn't be carrying a slotted spoon for collecting specimens and an assortment of plastic bags to put them in.

Although young Garry, a pale and slightly pop-eyed strawberry blond, packs only a slim quarter-century under his belt, he exhibits collecting instincts equal to the Malacologist's. He travels south and farther south to gather data for his graduate thesis in meteorology. Mornings and midnights, through calms and gales, through lifting, plunging seas that raise his Q-factor—Q for queasy—to a midscale 5, he pulls himself on deck, grabs a pipe to keep from falling overboard, and takes readings for wind speed and direction, barometric pressure, humidity, and the temperatures of air and water. But despite his intentions, he shows what weathermen are really made of—hope and inexactitude—by carrying that royal-blue umbrella.

Searching for sensible metaphors is as good a reason as any for being in this very odd part of the world. So, in an effort to find them, I look at the facts. Or, rather, I look at two sets of facts that coexist somewhat uneasily because, while one set stays put, the other is subject to alteration. It's far easier to get a grip on facts arising out of nature and history than it is to get hold of facts that spring from the human brow like some poor, mortal imitation of Athena. These mutable facts go by various names—guidelines, regulations, management plans. But here, to begin with, are some of the other, stay-put kind.

Invisible boundaries demarcate the subantarctic. These limits can nonetheless be clearly measured by shifts in the temperature and density of seawater. On the northern edge, the warm water of the Pacific, Atlantic, and Indian oceans meets the surface water of the Southern Ocean, which is consistently colder by more than seven degrees Fahrenheit; at this juncture, known as the subtropical convergence, the colder water sinks and circles back to the south. On the southern edge, or Antarctic convergence, these chilly seas collide with denser, even more frigid water, which in turn descends and curls back toward the perpetual ice at the bottom of the world.

Specks of land lie thinly scattered over the Southern Ocean's grey, globe-circling immensity, where summer sunlight glitters on the waves like frost. There are twenty-four groups of these tiny, uppity islands, born of volcanic eruptions and the slow grinding of tectonic plates and sculptured ever after by the constant abrasion of crashing seas and torrential rains. The islands, wrapped for millennia in stern, wave-guarded isolation, would have seduced Charles Darwin, had he sailed this far. Like the equator-straddling Galápagos Islands with their endemic finches, tortoises, and seagoing iguanas, each group in the far, wintry south has served as a nursery to life-forms—from penguins and plovers to giant flowers—found on its shores and nowhere else. New Zealand claims five island clusters—a full five-ring circus.

The Antipodes group is the most remote, lying 542 statute miles southeast of Bluff, the country's most southerly port. Due north of the Antipodes, just above the 48th parallel, rise the Bounty Islands, low-lying and bare of vegetation, their granite rocks dark as the backs of whales. Or so I am told by photographs, for these two naturally far-flung groups are also isolated by restrictions of human devising: landings on the Bounties only in winter, when a large breeding population of easily riled fur seals is occupied elsewhere; no landings at all on the Antipodes.

The very small ship follows the sea road to the other and more accessible three: first to the Aucklands, astride the 50th parallel and by far the largest of the island clusters; then to Campbell, at 52°53' south the closest to Antarctic ice; and last to the Snares, a trifling 130-mile cruise southwest of Bluff. The Snares rear out of the sea like the crashing and ruinous Symplegades. In the days before steam and the opening of the Panama Canal, when the poorly charted, storm-wracked subantarctic groups lay athwart major shipping lanes, they did indeed snare many a wooden ship and hapless mariner. Not the Snares, however, but the Antipodes claimed the final shipwreck, that of the four-masted French barque *Président Felix Fauré* in 1908.

Nor are the islands friendly to humankind in most other respects. In the two hundred years since the five clusters were variously discovered by European explorers—including the notable Captain Cook and the notorious Captain Bligh, whose ship gave its name to the Bounty Islands—people have paused on one or another shore. Some tried to settle. No one has managed to stay. The Maori, intrepid and far-sailing Polynesians who established the first human presence in New Zealand, were surely acquainted with the subantarctic, but not even they could tame such boggy, wave-lashed, gale-pummeled islands into a semblance of hospitality.

Nonetheless, two centuries—though hardly a blip on the planetary timescale—are quite long enough for people to have left considerable reminders of their presence: the castaway depots once stocked with provisions for shipwrecked seamen; the huddled nineteenth-century graves of starved mariners and would-be farmers; the coast-watching huts and lookouts manned during the Second World War. But all these are derelict, increasingly ramshackle, returning to earth.

Other dots and slashes of the human signature are carved more indelibly into the landscape. On the shore of a tucked-away inlet on Auckland Island, the *rata* forest still gapes where the slow-growing hardwoods were clear-cut in 1939 to provide fuel for the *Erlangen*, a German cargo ship making a getaway from unsympathetic New Zealand on the eve of the war. And writ much larger on the land is the presence of animals that would never have showed up in these parts without help, some of it intended, some not. House mice, cats, Norway rats—all these arrived as shipborne stowaways that went ashore and settled in, dining happily on native birds. Pigs, goats, sheep, cattle, and the tarnished-silver rabbits were landed with the laudable purpose of providing self-renewing stocks of meat for castaways and settlers, but in the absence of such human predation, these introduced browsers and grazers have satisfied their own hearty appetites by eating some native plants into oblivion.

These are some of the incontrovertible facts—bits of the past that present circumstances cannot change.

The islands, for all their harshness, are treasure islands. I gather up every sensation I can, from the sound of squabbling gulls to the sight of tiny spiders in half-hidden webs, from the coppery taste of sunshine to the sting of sleet. Here are troupes of penguins, clowns on land but consummate acrobats beneath the waves. Over here, crisply patterned black-and-white variations on the theme of cormorant. And here, lavender, gold, and rust-red petals nestled in emerald leaves, bouquet on bouquet of giant flowers.

Young Garry shares in the bounty, although his chosen portion is of another order. He pulls out a tape recorder, an item he carries as faithfully as the royal-blue umbrella, and pushes the play button. Ah, the rattle-clank of the very small ship's anchor chain as it tumbles out of the hawsehole. The twenty-five-horsepower thrumming of the Zodiac raft that ferries us from ship to land. The sizzle and slosh of rushing, receding waves. The Guide preaching the gospel of wild places and reciting the commandments for reverent behavior therein. Garry shakes his head and pushes fast-forward. His pale blue, slightly pop-eyed gaze twinkles; his smile is cherubic. "I should like you to hear the disgusting sea elephants," he says in a prim voice. "You wouldn't invite *them* for dinner." He speaks of the elephant seals he saw three hours ago—monstrous, blubbery bulls with pendulous and rumpled snouts. Breeding season over, they've come ashore where they settle in for several months to molt. They plop their several tons upon the earth and proceed to sink in the boggy soil, where they become marooned in deep, muddy wallows of their own excremental making. The tape plays. Again water swishes and fizzes, but this time the gentle sounds are accompanied by snorts and gargled groans, by regal eructations and positively imperial flatulence.

The Malacologist scrapes her treasure of mollusks off underwater rocks, scoops it up with bay-bottom sand, and takes it in bags to her cabin aboard the very small ship. Her cabinmate complains mildly, helplessly, about the pervasive chemical reek of preservatives. The Malacologist is not fazed. She has something else to worry about: what They with a capital *T* might do. "Do you suppose," she asks with palpable anxiety, "that They might confiscate the mollusks I have collected if They should find species not listed on my permit?"

So it is, with a flourish of permits and a gaggle of guidelines, that I arrive at the shifting, slippery, marvelous realm of facts concocted by the human brain. But their point of origin and Cheshire-cat ephemerality make them no less real—for their duration—than the facts afforded by geology, biology, and history. And even after such come-and-go facts have been supplanted in the current wisdom, the consequences of acting on them may be quite as lasting, quite as adamant as stone.

Though I'm not Alice, I may have fallen into Wonderland, or perhaps just down a hole dug by a rabbit with tarnished silver fur. That rabbit and its multitudinous kin are probably doomed, but more of that later.

On this voyage, the very small ship carries thirty-five people. The Guide has leased her, and ten of her usual crew are aboard. They more often sail the South Pacific as missionaries, delivering repairs to ailing bodies, aching teeth, and bedeviled souls. Five more crew members are present for the occasion, including the Guide, his sidekick the Wildlife Biologist, and the Captain, who once spent three years circumnavigating the south polar ice in a ten-meter yacht that he built himself. We passengers number nineteen—one Australian, one Scot, two Americans, and fifteen Kiwis, more men than women.

Nineteen passengers, fifteen on the crew—that's thirty-four. The thirty-fifth person aboard is our chaperone, our watchdog, our very own Rip. A slender, freckled, amiable young woman, she works in real life with the Protected Species Division of New Zealand's Department of

Conservation. The department—known as DoC, an acronym pronounced as if it had something to do with the medical profession—was
formed in 1987 of three overlapping agencies: the Forest Service, the
Wildlife Service, and the Department of Lands and Survey. The Rip is
more accurately DoC's representative, or rep, a syllable that slides with
a short *i* off Kiwi tongues. She embodies for us the mandate that a DoC
employee with subantarctic experience accompany every voyage to the
islands. Her job as Rip is to make sure that we do not import any plants
or animals (no dormice), nor bother the birds (no flamingos used as cro-
quet mallets), nor violate the other pronouncements of DoC (not to be
mistaken for the Red Queen).

Our Rip, I discover, has never before made a visit to Wonderland and,
despite the mandate, does not stay with us for the entire voyage. We're
put in charge of our own good behavior when she joins a DoC field team
making a census of bird populations on an island in the Aucklands that
has not yet been modified by humankind. The census is part of a much
greater head-counting effort meant to provide baseline statistics on
Wonderland's flora and fauna. The idea is that fragile ecosystems with
their indigenous plants and animals stand a somewhat better chance of
being kept safe from the onslaughts of *Homo sapiens* if we know what's
there and in what numbers.

And *Homo sapiens* is on the move south. This time, however, it's not explorers, castaway seamen, sealers and whalers, prospective settlers, and
coast watchers who travel the vast grey reaches of the Southern Ocean
to fetch up on one or another of a bunch of tiny islands. This time, for all
our attempts to dignify ourselves with serious names like Botanist or
Wildlife Photographer or Writer, most of us are really lower-case
tourists.

"I should really like to have a picture of this one," says the Malacologist. She holds up a plastic bag that contains a small, phlegmy, pale yellow glob.

She might as well be speaking to the air. There's no one in the ship's lounge but the two of us. The people who understand such things as speed groups, f-stops, filters, and telescopic lenses, who carry backpacks with specially constructed compartments for photographic equipment and supplies, are all somewhere else. Napping probably, for it's late afternoon, and they've spent the day trekking up and down several miles of those well-nigh vertical mountain bogs. Our Malacologist chose, of course, to remain at sea level collecting mollusks from the rocks of a placid cove. I've been on board nursing a sore shoulder wrenched several days ago as the ship rolled and pitched unsteadily on the twelve-meter swells. I flew off my feet and came down with a crash on the far side of the lounge.

"Come now, you have a camera," she says brightly. Nor will she accept my declarations of ineptitude. Then, because the glob cannot be properly photographed while it's squinched at the bottom of a bag, we must find some sort of dish to put it in. All that the moment provides in the way of a dish is one of the larger lens caps from my binoculars. The glob, bathed in seawater and pulsing almost imperceptibly, occupies no more than a fifth of its space. Ready, set, click! I snap three shots and ask her if she knows what manner of creature this creature is.

"Oh yes, a sea slug. But this one's unfamiliar, certainly not on my permit. It could be a subantarctic version of something rather ordinary, or it could be something entirely new."

She's much too excited to think of what They might do. And she may have realized that if They aim to protect birds, sea lions, and giant greenery, it behooves Them to learn as much as possible about pale yellow globs and how such trifles fit into the largely unstudied subantarctic scheme of things.

Campbell Island: I plod slowly toward Col Ridge.

Though the mile-long track—the only board walk in all the islands—floats above the oozy peat like a magic carpet, my sore shoulder and

creaky knees protest at being pushed ever upward from the meteorological station on the rocky shore of Beeman Cove, up around the forested
flank of Mount Beeman, and up across the herbfields above the tree line
where giant flowers lift gold and purple heads and bleached-white snow
grass grows in great, waist-high tussocks. With a quick flip of some ce-
lestial switch, the summer sun winks out and sleet drives horizontal on a
harsh wind. I pull up the hood of my oilskin and tug on my mittens. The
sun winks calmly on again. Hovering on the brink of retreat, I almost
turn to go back down again. But reward for effort and soreness awaits on
the ridge—the royal albatrosses on their nests. Onward and upward, it's
best to keep plodding.

These subantarctic island clusters must be among the wildest places
left on earth. The reason for such wildness is, of course, that they're in-
imical to my sort of two-legged beast. The only human beings who have
recently managed to live here on a continuing basis are the youthful
teams manning Campbell's meteorological station year-round and the
scientists camped in the Aucklands to study the population dynamics of
the Hooker's sea lions at Sandy Bay. The teams rotate every year, however, and the scientists heave in for the sea lions' summer breeding season and then heave home again. Nobody comes to the islands seeking to
take up permanent, lifelong residence.

But we tourists do come seeking—what? Adventure, certainly. Rare
sights. A nodding acquaintance with true wilderness. And, perhaps, an
element less easily defined, the whatever-it-is that the Guide calls the
"spiritual dimension" of our journey. A sense of awe? Of human finitude?

Trained as a wildlife biologist, the Guide is also an ordained Presbyterian minister. He has no church but leads his shipborne, ad hoc con-
gregations onto these specks of land, these lush and forbidding islands,
and here he preaches a gospel of wild places. In his ardent view, we are
not tourists on an ecocruise but folk on pilgrimage, headed toward some
Canterbury that's built of peat, flowers, and scrubby forest and set atop
craggy cliffs whence seabirds and wonder both take wing.

Slowly, knees aching, I make it to the top of Col Ridge. Here, as guaranteed, is the colony of nesting royal albatrosses. Along with the great bird that lets me know it knows I'm here with a clacking of its pale pink mandibles, at least a dozen other birds are visible at widely spaced intervals amid the tussocks, ferns, and giant greenery. And, like the summer sunshine giving way to wind and sleet—flicking on, then flicking off again—I am assailed by alternating sensations. A huge joy at being on this ridge is countered by a strong suspicion that I ought not to be here in the first place lest I contribute to the vanishing of all that affords me such joy.

Is a place best preserved by letting no one use it? Or should we use it at the risk of ruining everything worth preserving? Then common sense catches up with me. A dilemma exists, all right. But it can't be unknotted by being picked at with such bleak, either-or naiveté. The one true question may be, Where's the peaceable ground that can accommodate us all, natives and outlanders alike?

The need to discover harmony between conflicting requirements and desires arises everywhere. It arises not just on fragile islands guarded from most incursions by vast, grey, seasick distances but also along the shores of my wide and salty North Carolina river, the Neuse. There, timber plantations yield to real estate developments at the noticeable expense of quail, thrushes, and warblers; the gallonage of domestic and industrial wastes poured into the river increases every year, with mounting costs in toxic algal blooms and diseased marine life. It arises on the Virginia river of my growing up, the Bullpasture, where water welling clear from mountain springs is being traded off for the leachates from streamside poultry farms.

Later, as the sun sets, I'll tell the Guide that he's right, these islands feel like sacred ground. He'll say that there's never been anything wrong with visiting the holy places. No, nothing wrong there, but it's altogether another story when the bulls already running loose in the china shop are invited into the cathedral.

But here I am, nooning on a windy, bird-bright ridge, perhaps as close to pure empyreal bliss as I'll ever be. The hardier pilgrims are elsewhere, traipsing over hills and soggy dales for mile on trackless mile. But three of the Wildlife Photographers are here using up film at the rate of one roll every five minutes. Ignoring the albatrosses, two of the Botanists are peering intently at the life-styles of the megaherbs. And one of the Gadabouts, an elderly gentleman, is engaged in owlish concentration on his lunch—crackers and cheese, sandwiches, fruit, cartons of juice packed on board ship right after breakfast. He wears a Band-Aid across his nose, skinned raw in the same sort of tumble that gave my shoulder grief. Finding a spot more dry than wet, I sit beside him and dig right smartly into my own lunch.

The shuffle back down to the met station and the shore of Beeman Cove is easier by far than the upward plod. And there's our Malacologist at water's edge, easy to see in her white oilskins as she gathers mollusks from the glistening rocks.

Wonderland indeed, but the metaphor suggested by Canterbury may be closer to the one I'm seeking. Lord knows, we ecopilgrims are just as motley and antic as the group assembled long ago by Chaucer. The main difference may be that we latter-day travelers will never achieve our literary forebears' enduring fame.

Eyes twinkling, cherubic grin in place, young Garry announces, "Today at 1600, the water temperature here was 9.4 degrees."

It's 6:00 P.M. Dark waves lapping gently at her hull, the very small ship lies at anchor in Beeman Cove half a mile off the met station. Several of us, freshened up after the day's exertions, stand on deck watching the First Mate cast bread upon the waters—or, more accurately, bread and stale cookies, coffee grounds, orange peels, and similar scraps from the galley, over which the large black-backed Dominican gulls, the daintier red-billed (and red-legged) gulls, and the sooty-brown, garbage-loving giant petrels are making a flapping, screaming fuss.

"Approximately forty-nine of your degrees," says young Garry, noticing my trouble converting his Celsius to my Fahrenheit. "Ta-da! You see before you the mad swimmer of Beeman Cove."

I wasn't there, but I can see him all right—royal-blue swimming briefs, blue-white skin, goose bumps, chattering teeth. "You swam? Out there in water that's nearly an ice cube?"

Tremendously pleased with himself, he gives me a splash-by-splash replay. "I began by wading in. The seabed sloped in gradually, and there were a few rocks about. And, yes, I actually swam, made sure I went *right* under. Then I was in the water two full minutes. There was an initial cold shock when I first plunged in, but after that the body realizes that it's useless to continue sending pain signals to the brain. I got used to it. I would have stayed in five minutes, but the Zodiacs were returning to the ship, and I didn't want to miss the boat."

Canterbury—well, perhaps. But another metaphor suggests itself when I'm back on the South Island mainland and meet the man to whom the Guide cordially refers as the Ayatollah. I'll be more polite and call him the Bureaucrat. But first, it may be well to say a few words about such things as Zodiacs and the guidelines bearing DoC's imprimatur and some of the other devices employed to open the islands to human use and, at the same time, protect them from overuse.

As in the Galápagos, these islands have no wharves at which a ship may tie up. No wharves, no mooring lines, no handy-dandy gangplanks for undesirable alien rodents. (Our very small ship is not the only pilgrim-bearing vessel that sails these waters; several much larger tour ships also make the subantarctic rounds. One, built in Russia, began her career as an icebreaker. Another, launched in 1991, caters to the comfort of well-heeled ecocruisers with such amenities as stabilizers, swimming pool, sauna, gaming tables, and live music for dancing.) Zodiacs, the inflatable, aluminum-reinforced rafts favored by such as Jacques-Yves Cousteau, furnish the only means of reaching shore. When the very small ship drops her anchor, we swaddle ourselves in blaze-orange life jackets, clamber down into a raft, and ride six or eight at a time to our landing. More often than not, it's a wave-washed, slippery stretch of cobblestones rather than a sandy beach.

And I learn that I can fly—at least for short distances. Even at the best of times, I lack agility and balance. The only way for me to manage a landing here is to stretch out my arms, sore shoulder notwithstanding. Two sturdy volunteers grab hold and whisk me through the air.

Once ashore, we find no conveniences—no trash cans, no toilets, no shelters from wind and rain, no overnight accommodations. Nor is camping allowed except by special permit, and then only for people engaged in serious research—counting the albatrosses, studying sea lions. We tourists wear our shelters in the form of oilskins and rubber boots. We pack our empty film containers, candy and sandwich wrappers, juice cartons, peach pits, and banana peels back to the floating hotels moored half a mile offshore. In times of need we duck behind a tussock or a tree fern (in the more visited Galápagos, human wastes are not allowed to sully earth but must be captured in plastic bags and carried back to the tour ship). On reboarding the ship, we wash our boots so that seeds and soil-borne microorganisms from one island won't be transported to the next.

Sometimes, though, we board the Zodiacs but make no landing. Instead, as at the Snares, we bounce along offshore to see what can be seen. Fur seals bask on shoreside rocks or sport amid the long, rubbery, yellow-brown strands of bull kelp. Endemic erect-crested penguins, stocky birds with stout orange bills and twizzles of yellow feathers over their eyes, pop in and out of the water like jumping jacks. Darting from shadow to shadow, a small brown fernbird shows itself for an instant; the feathers of its long, stiff-spined tail are as frayed as the silk of an antique fan.

Landing or just looking—the determination is made according to the extent that each island remains pristine or nearly so or has been modified, sometimes greatly, in the two centuries since people became aware of these odd little places. So, it has been decreed that the untouched islands are off-limits except to scientific field teams, and some—but not all—of those already damaged may be further, though discreetly, tramped upon. Discretion has to do with placing stern restrictions on the number of people who may do the tramping. DoC's official Guidelines on Tourism state: "Maximum of 600 people will be permitted to land at any one designated tourist site per year." Compare that to twenty-some thousand, the annual limit that Ecuador sets on visits to the Galápagos. But there's no land rush to the subantarctic, no pushing and shoving, for the lucky six hundred are further divided into groups of no more than thirty, often fewer, who are allowed ashore at any one time.

The guidelines also instruct us most reasonably not to smoke while ashore, leave any rubbish, take specimens without a permit, or collect souvenirs. And they adjure us "to protect wildlife and avoid violating the seals', penguins', or seabirds' personal space." Animals always have the right of way, and we may go no closer than fifteen feet to seabirds, twenty feet to marine mammals. But if sea lion cows issue invitations to play? Or the pups wriggle over our feet? Or penguins come waddling over to stare? We do not break DoC's commandments. The animals, quite unfettered by notions of should and should not, have freely entered *our* personal space.

The guidelines, though always subject to being ignored, selectively interpreted, or fiddled with, make good sense. They establish a code of manners for visitors. They allow a representative sampling of the subantarctic's harsh, green loveliness. Though all sorts of people, from scientists to pilgrims to curiosity seekers, are spilling south, the islands seem to be safe from poachers, loggers, squatters, graffiti artists, and similar vandals. And there's a movement afoot that would heal some of the damage and bring selected environments back to a state resembling Eden. Or so I think before I meet the Bureaucrat.

But I don't meet him until our band of travelers has returned from Beeman Cove to South Island's firm ground. The northward voyage takes thirty-six rolling, pitching, heaving, and plunging hours. As on the jour-

ney south, walking across the lounge from settee to head and back is a
dangerous proposition; some of the less acrobatic tough it out and tumble, others (I among them) say to hell with dignity and scuttle safely
along on hands and knees. But we've all found our sea legs. We're all smiling, all brimming over with grateful amazement. Young Garry wears the
broadest grin of all. It looks as if he's hugging a secret, but it could be that
our swimmer is just plain happily, madly full of himself.

A glory of seabirds fills the huge grey sky. Around the very small ship
in every direction, thousands on thousands of far-ranging birds wheel
and soar—gleaming great albatrosses and their not-much-smaller kin the
mollymawks, the boldly patterned black-and-white petrels known as
cape pigeons, and dark shearwaters cutting through the waves, tiny pri-
ons dancing on the glitter of the surface. Dusky dolphins, riding our bow
wave, escort us almost all the way to home port.

Suddenly, the ground of South Island isn't firm, and the place to which
I am transported is one that Captain Lemuel Gulliver would readily appreciate. He suffered many a shipwreck on the wilder shores of obfusca-
tion and absurdity. Forget L. Frank Baum, Lewis Carroll, and Geoffrey
Chaucer. None other than Jonathan Swift has provided the proper
metaphor by which facts of the mutable sort may be understood. My role,
however, is not that of Gulliver. No indeed. I am a genuine Yahoo.

But it does not occur to me beforehand that this is part of what I'll
learn when I go to see the Bureaucrat. A dark, talkative man with the ample, well-fed look of a sea lion, he is a servant of DoC both as Habitat and
Fauna Officer for his region and as the middle member of a three-man
team entrusted with subantarctic management. Like many of his kind, he
exhibits tendencies to hide behind verbosity, rely on ritual jargon, and
answer questions with chapter and verse. His texts for these citations are
five management plans, one for each island group, and his monologues
are studded with terms like "the conservation estate," "business planning
system," "risk management," "learning curve," and "cost recovery."

Cost recovery? "Yih," he says. That's kiwi for "yeah," and almost everyone, not just the Bureaucrat, says it that way. I learn that DoC, working
with a budget that has been cut back each year since the department's in-
ception in 1987, is required to generate or recover some twenty percent
of its annual operating costs. One stratagem is that of charging for the
permits that allow the lucky six hundred to visit the subantarctic. For
larger ships such as the former icebreaker, a day-by-day fee is set according to the size of the vessel; for smaller ships like ours, it is levied,
through the tour operator, on each individual tourist. Nothing amiss
with charging an entrance fee, I think, until the Bureaucrat says, "We're
relying on those tour ships to meet our revenue targets."

Risk management? When we bounced in a Zodiac along the rugged
shores of the Snares—the nearly pristine Snares, where nary a rat has
been introduced to devour the eggs of burrow-dwelling petrels and nary
a pig to root up tender plants—I noticed stout ropes connected to some
shoreside rocks. I learn that these are moorings—been there for years—
at which rock-lobster fishermen tie up their boats. Of course, as the Bureaucrat tells me, the fishing boats do put the Snares at risk, but risk is
minimized because DoC has not only issued permits for the moorings
but also set the strictest conditions on their use. No Rip in sight, the fishermen (and any stowaways) observe the honor system.

But when the Bureaucrat says that the highest management priority is
to prevent further damage to the islands, I can give heartfelt assent. More
than that, if it seems that some existing damage might be reversed, then
there should be all-out efforts to bring the islands back to something resembling their original, untrammeled state. And, truly, some notable
restoration has already been achieved. Take Campbell Island's sheep, feral survivors of attempts at sheep farming from the 1890s to the early
1930s. For decades they nibbled away at the vegetation and nibbled
much of it right down to the ground. But now that the twenty-first century is coming and the last of the sheep have finally fallen to the gun,

grasses and flowering plants once thought to have been lost forever spring up again. I can easily cheer such planning and implementation.

Until, that is, I check up on a rumor I've heard about the rabbits of Enderby Island in the Aucklands, those rabbits with fur the color of tarnished silver. They have inhabited the island for a hundred years and share its lawnlike greensward, its gnarled forests with the immemorial Hooker's sea lions and yellow-eyed penguins. In line with a policy of removing introduced mammals wherever possible, they're slated for "taking," as the Bureaucrat puts it. That means extermination. There's no doubt that the rabbits, an old-fashioned French breed called *Argenté de Champagne*, have wreaked considerable havoc during their short tenure. The *rata* forest has retreated under assault from sharp rabbit incisors, which have also created the short-cropped sward. Sea lion pups sometimes fall into rabbit burrows, where they become trapped and die. I've seen these depressions filled with small white bones. Just about all the rabbits are good for is food—occasional dinners for the scientists studying the sea lions, quotidien prey for the skua, a large, rapacious bird that stalks and pounces. But it strikes me that killing Enderby's myriad rabbits is an iffy proposition at best, and I say so. The Bureaucrat responds that the only question here is not, Can we really hope to wipe them out? It's, When they're gone, to what extent will the island recover? So far, so good. If a choice must be made, it's a safe bet that most people would opt for pups over bunnies. And how will the plan be implemented? The Bureaucrat shrugs and, for once, says nothing at all. But thousands of rabbits can't be easily trapped, much less gunned down like sheep. The Guide and his sidekick the Wildlife Biologist have already mentioned the method: a poison called 1080, Ten-Eighty.

Later I check with my veterinarian-daughter on its nature. That's a brand name, she says, for sodium monofluoroacetate, a poison developed to control rodents and insect pests. Colorless, odorless, soluble, it is a nonselective, highly toxic substance that goes up the food chain.

There is no antidote. Its use is banned in the United States except by federal license, for which a state government may apply in order to kill, say coyotes. And then the stuff must be mixed with black dye so that the people spreading it around can see it.

Yih.

But even as I'm talking with the Bureaucrat, I realize that it's not entirely his fault that I've begun to locate subantarctic islands in Swiftian realms, to see them as Lilliput and Blefuscu, Laputa, Balnibarbi, and ghostly Glubbdubdribb. I've somehow stopped seeing the islands' physical truth and started noting, with bemusement, how these specks of rock have been swaddled and veiled in a patchwork of human notions. But the Bureaucrat didn't piece and stitch this crazy quilt all by himself. Much of the fabric comes with his job. And he is engaged in a quest, reaching out and grabbing, just as I am, for ways of putting some tender, sopping, brutal, quite magical places into a context that he can cope with. Though his language is charmless, reductive, and trucked in wholesale from some jargon junkyard, he's striving for a good and necessary goal, even though he's going about it upside down, inside out, and bass-ackward.

But the Swiftian lens that I've been peering through doesn't bring the situation into clear focus either. And I begin to suspect that the proper metaphors for understanding subantarctic islands have not been discovered by anyone anywhere. They may not exist. Not yet.

How naked the islands are. The forests rustle dark green beneath the wind, and the birds explode upward, wings beating the air, from nests atop cliffs and nests burrowed deep in the ground. But the islands themselves are naked and blind as featherless chicks. No legends invest them, no myths, no cosmologies. They are entirely innocent of the constructs of faith, imagination, and desire.

Apart from the Poles, the starkest mountains, and the great deserts, few parts of the planet are so forbidding that no one can live there. People have managed to earn, or eke out, their livings in almost every climate and terrain, from the Arctic to the Australian outback, from dusty prairies to steamy rain forests dripping with orchids and leeches. In the thousands of places that people have made themselves at home for thousands of years, the land is always dressed up in songs and stories. And the earth that is tilled or hunted over, that witnesses the births and weddings and burials of generation after human generation, gains an invisible dimension.

The land itself shimmers with sacredness, like the glowing of a banked fire or the sparkle of moonlight on snow, on swift-running water. The land's physical features acquire a history, telling how heaven connects with the earth: Here is the mountain where god was born, here the cave that leads to the underworld, and here the gully where mortals rose up out of the excreta—blood, tears, sweat, or shit—of some divine accident. If these tangible places and things, and the dangerously holy world they represent, should be profaned, their capacities for real and psychic nurturance abused or wasted, then as surely as big fish eat little ones, some timeless, wrathful energy will snap up the puny transgressors and swallow them whole.

But just as the sacred places hold cursing and death, they also hold blessing and life. We become poets and priests, responding to their numen with stories and songs, dances, ceremonies, prayers, and all that will ease our passage from one stage of life to the next and keep us peaceful with the spirits in the land. Here is the bare and rocky butte that a boy must climb so that he may fast and dream his man's name. Here is the fresh-flowing water with which a woman purifies herself of the blood of menstruation or childbirth. Here is the graveyard where the sleeping ancestors wait for some last, victorious trump.

The ocean at the bottom of the world is holy and inhabited by a deity—the god that the Maoris call Tangaroa. And in these waters I have seen a fishing boat that tried to cover the possibilities by wearing (just in case) the name *San Tangaroa* on bow and stern. That's tantamount to calling a vessel the *Saint Poseidon*. But the rocky islands that thrust heavenward out of the cold, grey sea have made only a faint obtrusion on human awareness during the past two hundred years, and no one has ever been able to settle in and stay.

I subscribe to the archaic Greek conviction that everything is sacred in its own right. Everything, and that means sea lions, albatrosses, tarnished-silver rabbits, *rata* trees, and giant purple flowers, oozy peat, the Malacologist's pale yellow glob, and dozens upon dozens of other miracles, including the Guide, the Bureaucrat, and eager young Garry. Nor does it matter if the object be alive or dead, or if it never lived at all. My list, therefore, falls short without such items as bleached sea lion bones, wave-rounded rocks, sleet driven hard on a howling summer wind, and, yes, young Garry's blue umbrella.

The bursting ecophilia of the present moment recovers some of that view of the world and also some of the old Greek emphasis on *kairos*—balance or moderation. A sampling of islands, with rips and guides, gadabouts and pilgrims limited to six hundred—that's *kairos* in action. And it's easy to agree with the thesis that there's a spiritual dimension to every part of the natural world. But let agreement be felt as well as reasoned. It's the heart that transforms an idea into an article of faith. And for some of us, it may take a continuing human presence to infuse a place with sanctity, to imagine its gods and commandments, and to honor them.

How vulnerable, these lovely, unlivable scraps of subantarctic rock. Nothing in human thought or experience has yet hallowed them. And they have no voices of their very own, no Moses, Homer, Aristotle, nor even a Thoreau.

But subantarctic dreams rise up like birds in hope's pure white air. They swim in hope's cold waters like gleaming fish and great sleek seals.

The Malacologist has brought home 126 species of mollusk. The pale yellow glob turns out to be no true sea slug but a creature with a small residual shell. She puts a mellifluous name to it—*Lamellaria nodosa*. But a full twenty-two of the 126 have never before been collected in the subantarctic. Perhaps they are found in other waters. Then again, perhaps they aren't!

The Mad Swimmer has certainly found his name. He may have found his country too. He announces that he's decided not to emigrate to Australia after all. And he's made a tape of subantarctic sounds, from the Guide's wild-places gospel, the slap-crash of waves on the very small ship's hull and the rattle of her anchor chain to—of course—the belches and farts of the elephant seals. And—oh, listen to this but don't tell— there's a girl.

It may be that the legends by which the islands live or die are in the making.

the waters
of night

"If you look over the railing, down inside, you can see a large, white, lighted column? This is known as Pluto's Ghost?"

Our guide's every sentence ends with a lift that turns the words into a question. She's leading us through Luray Caverns. Underground for ten minutes now, we wend our way down beneath the earth's surface on a wide brick pathway, with duly scheduled pauses to admire the Ghost and other dramatically floodlit formations. Our tour group is tiny, not the usual summertime horde, but only eight altogether, including the guide. Such elbowroom, such luxurious privacy, are accounted for by the season. It's the lull just before Christmas, when proper tourists stay close to the fire and dream of August vacations.

"Pluto is the name of the Roman god of the underworld? And the reason why it's called Ghost is because you keep on seeing the same formation a total of three times? And it seems to haunt or follow you like a ghost would?"

The Ghost wears a gleaming toga of finely pleated stone. We look at the slender column, stalactite joined to stalagmite, then move along at a leisurely pace.

On the theory that schoolbook facts are well served by real-world examples, I've brought my granddaughter Melissa, aged eleven, and her friend Hilda to Luray for their first-ever excursion beneath the earth. (Oh, all right, the girls are my excuse for coming here, for treating myself to yet another tour, at least the fourth, of this particular labyrinth.) By the time we encounter the spectral column, the guide has given us an overview of history and geology.

We've heard about the caverns' discovery in the summer of 1878 by several men who knew what they were looking for in this region of sinkholes and soluble limestone—a subterranean attraction that might entice free-spending visitors to an always poor rural area impoverished even further by the Civil War. A short three months later, the caverns were opened to the public. Melissa and Hilda are not much interested in such information, but I'll tell them later how darkness was banished so that the public could view the underworld in a day without electric lights; I've read about the magnesium flares and seen old drawings of torches leaning out from the walls and candelabra suspended from the tips of stalactites. Two days after Christmas in 1878, six hundred paying visitors—ladies in bustles, gentlemen in frock coats and bowler hats—descended to the large chamber known as The Ballroom, where they took refreshment and danced to the music of a band hired expressly for the grand occasion.

We've heard about the human bones found in the alley now known as Skeleton's Gorge. They belonged to a teenaged girl, probably a Native American, and fell through a sinkhole sometime after her burial on the surface. The Smithsonian stores them now. "Oooo," say Melissa and Hilda, making faces.

We're told that geologists estimate the caverns' age at 400 million years, and we see the dripstone—the stalactites and stalagmites that have accreted drop by drop over that incomprehensible span of time. Some are still growing; water glistens at their tips and tops and down their sides. Soon we'll encounter flowstone—smooth coatings deposited layer by thin layer as water flows over ceilings and walls. Sometimes the flowstone hangs down in folded, translucent, forever frozen curtains called draperies. And we hear about the colors in the formations—white for calcium, an ashy grey for magnesium, an orange-red for iron. "Cool!" say Melissa and Hilda, and "Neat!"

We're instructed not to touch anything, nor try to break off souvenirs. When Melissa and Hilda want to know why, the guide informs us that the caverns are protected by state law. Touching leaves behind skin oils, which can discolor stone and, worse, stop a formation's growth. I remember, however, that once upon a time not very long ago—within the last decade, in fact—visitors were encouraged near tour's end to rub their fingers across the Two Fried Eggs for luck. But when I ask about touching these slender, broken-off stalagmites that are definitely sunny-side up in color and size, the guide shakes her head and says, "Once maybe? Not anymore."

The tour of wonderland takes us past the shallow reflecting pool of Dream Lake; past the intricate filigrees, the layered wedding cakes of Totem Pole Valley; past the delicate and never-moving draperies of Saracen's Tent; past the massive Fallen Stalactite, which an earthquake shook from the ceiling seven millennia ago; past the gargantuan columns of Giants' Hall; and into the great room called the Cathedral, where electrically activated hammers with rubber tips strike formations, selected by an English tuning fork, to play slow tunes. We're told that the contraption is an organ, but it's not, for the sound does not depend on pipes and air. It's a percussion instrument, a great xylophone, made not of wood but petrified water, that covers three acres. In keeping with the season, we're given a carol. But the music is soft and plaintive, almost timid. Even "Silent Night" cannot compete with the vaulted immensity of this room and the fluent, swirling darkness that presses damp and close around the little pool of light in which we stand.

I feel as heavy as yonder stone. . . . Beside the rivering waters of, hitherandthithering waters of. Night!

The waters of night flow underground at Luray. Just as they rush and babble and tumble through the landscape of *Finnegans Wake* and carve new courses through language, I'm sure that the waters of night also scour great channels for themselves everywhere under the earth. Welling moonless and star-bereft out of some grotesque, abyssal silence, they fill and overflow every available subterranean cranny and chamber. Here be dragons, here tigers and terrors. Here everything conjured by hitherandthithering thought becomes palpable—not seen or heard necessarily, but present all the same, hiding and waiting to pounce. Only outermost space might contain a darkness more unbounded and fantastic. Did James Joyce ever go underground? Did he ever set foot and imagination inside a cave?

Oh, the caves of the world! Mountain caves carved by trickles and seeps, sea caves hammered out by waves, caves within lava or glacial ice. Caves that shimmer with the light of glowworms; caves with lightless streams that harbor blind, white fish; caves from which a thousand thousand bats stream forth at dusk. Caves with walls on which the painted cattle, deer, and bison still magically invite the spears and projectiles of long-dead hunters. Caves that serve as regal halls for the mountain king, or store stolen treasure for Ruggedo, monarch of every gnome beneath Oz. Fusty caves smelling of mildew, uncured hides, and the smoke of old fires, in which the centaurs—Kheiron, for one—tutor the striplings, like Achilles, who will grow to be heroes. Holy caves where god-ridden women babble prophecies not just of things to come but of things that already are. Heart-stopping caves with passageways that slope precipitously down and down from living, daylit realms into the clotted, never-ending darkness of the underworld.

The Roman poet Virgil tells of Aeneas' fearful descent into just such a cave, the cave at Cumae on Italy's west coast. He entered that haunt of night to learn the fate of Rome, the city he was destined to found. And along with the narrative of his hero's journey into the regions below, Virgil bequeaths us a description of the cave. It opens to the upperworld on the face of a great cave-pocked cliff, and through its hundred entrances, its hundred mouths, the responses of the prophetess whose home it is come rushing forth. Inside the gaping maw of the main portal, the cave is immense, its floor rocky underfoot, its roof out of reach. The almost measureless spaces are guarded by a dark lake and a shadowy forest. Nothing flies here, no bird is safe, so poisonous the breath that rises from the jaws of a black chasm.

The wildest of wild caves, that one—night's ultimate reservoir. In such buried places, imagination goes feral, and the lightless waters quietly surge up and drown all reason. How tame in comparison, how docile, the caverns at Luray. But then, their darkness has been domesticated for more than a century. It's been contained behind man-made dams—illuminated walkways, iron railings, and pet names for the most imposing formations.

Once, alone and inspired by damn foolishness, I crawled into an untamed cave. The place, Vermont; the time, four decades ago, on a mild grey day early in the spring. The adventure came about because the pro-

fessor who taught my introductory course in geology mentioned a local
cave that was not widely known, not large, certainly not scheduled for a
field trip, but nonetheless—his word—spectacular. How could I not include caving on my list of projects good for redeeming an otherwise aim-
less afternoon?

When the afternoon arrived, I bundled against all possible chills in
parka and scarf, mittens, and zippered rubber stadium boots topped with
fake fur. Under my blue jeans I wore bright red long johns. Grabbing a
flashlight, off I went in an old, mud-spattered black Ford borrowed from
a friend. With dairy farms on either side and Green Mountains looming
winter-dark in the background, I drove down a graveled country road.
The trees were beginning to show fat buds, but the grass was still brown,
and snow, resisting the season, sulked in bleak pockets. Wild ducks descended and settled on a farm pond that reflected the sky's drab greyness
but somehow made it shine.

The cave was situated within the low hump of a cleared hill that was
part of somebody's pasture. Its mouth opened, black and roughly trian-
gular, just yards from the road. I trespassed merrily—no permission had
been asked—through stiff spears of grass, over a sagging post-and-wire
fence, across the pasture's soggy turf. I had to stoop just a little to enter
the cave, but after the first few feet, the ceiling slanted sharply downward, and the only way to progress was on hands and knees. A miner's
helmet would have been useful. It's not easy to crawl while holding a
flashlight.

The geological details of that cave elude memory. I can't say now
what kind of rock it was, nor in what unimaginably ancient sea the sedi-
ments that became rock were first laid down. I do recall that the walls
were dark and intricately fractured. And they were wet. Moisture trickled down everywhere and collected in a rivulet that soaked my mittens
and the legs of my jeans. Water seeped through the furry tops of my stadium boots. A spring-fed trickle in tiny but constant flow? Meltwater
from the recent thaw? It hardly mattered. What counted was the pres-

ence of water. Over the cave's millennia, water had done its work well, dissolving rock as drop after tiny drop trickled down the walls in an insistent search for sea level. I had enough room at this point to kneel upright, head bent slightly against the ceiling, outspread elbows touching the walls.

The tunnel twisted, closed in more tightly, and branched. It made a Y with arms spread so wide it was almost a T. Taking either arm meant advancing on my belly. Turn back? Hardly. I had no reason to suppose that the professor of geology was not trustworthy; if he had pronounced the cave spectacular, there must be something to see other than wet rock. Around the next corner? I took the arm that seemed larger and more able to accommodate broad, professorial shoulders.

Parka now soaked, I slithered on. Nothing. It might be that spectacle lay in the eye of the beholder. It might be that the eye of a trained geologist had found some stunning opulence where mine found only rocks and water. I moved forward.

Then the roof of the cave raised itself a few inches, and the tunnel took a sharp turn. I angled the upper half of my body around the corner and lifted the flashlight. Cave's end. Partway up the far wall was a recessed hollow with its ledge curving toward me. Water glistened, caught on the lip of the curve like pale wine in a full-to-brimming cup. A mirror of water, and the reflection it held was a city in white crystal, a city out of a dream, all towers and spires. And above the water, like stars, shone the reason for this perfect architecture: delicate, faceted stalactites, none longer than my little finger and far less thick. In answer to the flashlight's beam, they threw off sparks, showers, cascades of scintillating light.

I don't know how long I stayed there almost holding my breath, gazing but not touching, not daring to put a brief human finger on such wonderwork. I did stay long enough to learn that the reflecting pool held life in the form of threadlike organisms that were nearly transparent because their generations had never known the sun.

The light of my own battery-powered sun dimmed from white to yellow. Time to leave, but the stricture of the tunnel left no room to turn around. Making an exit was a matter of rolling my clumsy, sodden self this way and that, of using my toes to pull me out backwards an inch at a time. All went well until I reached the Y. Left, right, which arm to take? Before I'd reached a decision, the flashlight failed. *Never enter a cave alone.* I'd broken the spelunkers' cardinal rule. I'd forgotten to take a spool of thread into the labyrinth, and there were minotaurs at large. The wet, cold, shuddering darkness rose in a flood and pinned me tightly against the tunnel's walls.

It should have been easy to find the way out, but I lay there unable to move in that numb, heart-pounding blackness. There were two ways to go, and both were wrong. Would there be rescue? No, not till another damn fool came crawling in, on a quest for something spectacular. And that might take years, a decade, a century. Desperation finally gave a galvanic shove. Light existed somewhere in the world, and if I wanted to see it again, I had to find it on my own. Inching backwards, I found it on the first try.

Please, oh please! Melissa and Hilda are asking me for coins. Our guide has led us to the Wishing Well. As far as the girls are concerned, it won't do to leave without making a wish and sealing it with a penny, a dime, or whatever I might be coaxed to come up with. The loot at the bottom of the well is scooped out once a year with hands and shovels, put into a bank account to gather interest, and later donated to nonprofit organizations. Please, pretty please! I hand each girl a quarter.

We're almost at tour's end. We've walked a bit more than a mile beneath the earth. It hasn't been an arduous trek, but, clad for chill December in the world above, I'm overdressed for conditions below. The caverns' temperature is constant year-round at fifty-four degrees, with an equally constant humidity of eighty-seven percent. No wonder my face is as beaded with moisture as these rock walls—I'm sweating.

Our small procession comes to a stop, and the guide says, "Now this plaque was placed here to recognize the men from Page County who have died in various wars? Since it is a small county, it means you don't get recognized very often—so, the plaque was placed here where about half a million people come through a year and see it. Now you'll have a few stairs to climb, and your tour is over?"

Melissa and Hilda make it to the gift shop before I've trudged even halfway up the steps. As they flit in agonies of indecision among post-cards, T-shirts, earrings, stuffed animals, and boxes made of aromatic cedar, I compare today's excursion with my earlier ventures into the sub-terranean, almost subaqueous regions of Luray. The tour itself has stayed the same, but the guide's commentary has been subtly altered. In this lat-est version of the spiel, facts have taken a slight edge over fancy. The ap-propriate technical terms, such as draperies, flowstone, dripstone, have bumped the cute and silly names once bestowed on a few of the more at-tention-grabbing formations. No longer is a stout stalagmite with a lump on top pointed out as Snoopy's Doghouse, nor is one particularly showy and translucent drapery now identified as Strips of Bacon. And the no-touch rule, only recently enforced, creates a new dividing line, almost a barricade, between flesh and stone, between the temporal and the timeless.

But Pluto's Ghost will persist, and Pluto's Chasm, Saracen's Tent, Totem Pole Valley. Many, the uses of metaphor, and some of them are splendid. Metaphor can lead to strange, rich insights by illuminating con-nections between objects that seem to be disparate or utterly incompat-ible. It might seem, however, that its commercial applications patronize intelligence and, worse, trivialize the phenomena on which such monikers are slapped. But there's purpose in the pet names bestowed on natural phenomena. The names, along with soft illumination, play com-forting tricks, persuading visitors that the underworld is almost a cozy place. Not so. Luray is not tame at all. It's quite wild, and the lights are marvelous devices—deceptions, really—that calm night's waters and keep them at bay. And the names attempt to reshape in human proportions things otherwise too huge to grasp—the uncountable millennia, the incomprehensibly powerful natural forces that wear away rock and rebuild it. Without the names that intercede and mediate, we'd be engulfed.

Melissa and Hilda are ready to go, to head with all speed for the nearest hamburgers, french fries, and milkshakes. And what have they purchased? Nothing at all. It may be simply that consuming food has become more urgent than consuming material goods, or it may be that they want to keep the money I gave them to splurge with. But perhaps, having gazed on wonders, they see the gift shop's offerings as out of keeping, as downright tawdry.

After lunch, on the long drive home, I itch to tell Melissa and Hilda about the Blue Grotto of Capri, the painted caves at Lascaux and Altamira, and Carlsbad Caverns with its million bats. I'd tell them about Cumae, too—how Aeneas entered the realm of the dead and came back alive. But the girls are playing with Barbie dolls and singing the latest pop songs in breathy, kid voices.

In the middle of a phrase, Melissa stops singing. "Grandma," she says in a most imperious tone, "you are going to take us there again."

the reports from the river styx

the River Styx is not a myth. It's not a figment of poetic imagination. Nor is it a metaphor for the stark dividing line between life and death. No one can dabble fingers and toes in a metaphor and get them wet. The time has come to set the record straight.

For at least three thousand years, the Styx, its tributaries, and their environs have been the subjects of much infernal rumor. Homer presents one topographic map, Virgil quite another; Dante and Milton offer their own distinctive charts. It's clear, however, that none of these reporters has visited the region, though Dante would have you believe that he made the journey with Virgil as his personal guide. If they had actually seen the Styx and its environs, we might expect closer conformity in their accounts. Living at different times, speaking different languages, they have all nonetheless written about one and the same place. But as matters stand, their material is disparate and finds little agreement except for a general coincidence in the names attached to the main features of the landscape. Unanimity occurs on only one point: that the Styx and its river systems are located in the netherworld. The exact metes and bounds are not provided.

A simplified map of the region may be drawn by sorting through and reconciling the variant accounts given by Homer, Virgil, and other ancient writers. Tartarus, as many writers have called the place, is bounded on the west by the River Styx, the Hated River. The ghosts of the newly dead gather on the west bank of the Styx and wait to be ferried across by Charon, who insists on payment before he lets them board his boat. But if a body has been buried without a small coin—the price of a ticket—under its tongue, the ghost must stay forever on the near shore, along with the ghosts of those not granted proper burial but carelessly left for the vultures and the dogs. The near bank sizzles and hums with the faint but unceasing protests of those who are stranded forever.

It may be further surmised from the old stories that at least four other rivers, and possibly five, flow into the Styx: Acheron, the River Woe; the Burning River, Phlegethon; the Wailing River, Cocytus, with water made salty by the tears of criminals; and the River of Forgetting, Lethe. Some say that Lethe's water is drunk so that the dead may mercifully forget what it was to be alive; others have it that the water also wipes out the memory of death in those souls worthy of being reborn. The fifth river, which does not figure in all accounts, is Avernus, the sulphurous stream beside which Virgil's hero Aeneas plucks the golden bough that will buy him passage out of the lightless underworld back into heaven's bright air. (To document the ease with which imagination appropriates features of the familiar upperworld, it may be noted that Avernus is also the ancient name of a lake situated near Naples, Italy.)

Tartarus, which is ruled by an absolute, divine authority known variously as Hades, Dis, or Pluto, consists of three separate jurisdictions. The ghosts who manage to cross the Styx are judged on arrival and sent to one or another of the three, according to the ways in which they conducted their earthly lives. The ghosts of everyday, middle-of-the-road folks, those people whose petty kindnesses balanced out their little white lies, are allowed to flutter forever, like wisps of early morning fog, in the Asphodel Meadows, which lie immediately on the Styx's far bank. Those whose crimes have offended gods and men are condemned to everlasting punishment in Tartarus proper. (It is this jurisdiction for which we have the best reports of distinct physical features: the lake from which the husband-murdering Danaids forever carry water in leaky jars; the slippery talus slope up which Sisyphos, betrayer of heavenly secrets, endlessly pushes a boulder; the swimming hole, canopied with fruit-laden boughs and vines, where everlasting hunger and thirst plague Tantalos, who not only slaughtered his son but served him up to the gods as the main course at dinner.) The third jurisdiction, reserved for those whose living deeds shone bright with virtue, is the paradisiacal Elysian Fields, which, as Homer describes them in the *Odyssey*, sound something like Hawaii—a place where black frosts and blizzards are quite unknown, a realm of dreamlike ease and endless summer, where a breeze like a soothing caress wafts always off the ocean, and winds like the trades blow fair and steady out of the west.

Nor is dying the only way to get to Tartarus. In addition to his sketchy description of the place, Homer presents an open-sesame formula, first given to Odysseus by the nymph Circe, by which the living may gain admittance to the regions below. According to ancient accounts, the

Styx basin, with its three political divisions, was the destination of choice for an elite and self-selected few. These travelers included in their number not only Odysseus and Aeneas but Theseus, who founded Athens, and the hero Herakles. And why would anybody in his right mind want to visit such a place? We're given many reasons: Aeneas desired one last conversation with his beloved father, and Herakles was following do-or-die orders for the capture of the three-headed dog that snarled and lunged on the Hated River's far bank. Odysseus himself, recipient of Circe's formula, entered the region to learn from the prophet Teiresias if he'd ever make it home to Ithaka. Such classical descents into Tartarus occurred, I am certain, not just for reasons of business but because of the same inquisitive awe that later sent pilgrims thronging on holy journeys to see the bloody garments, bony scraps, and mummified fingers of saints. For some, the urge to cross the Styx—not only cross it but come back to tell the tale—may well have been prompted by the same it's-there-so-I'll-do-it challenge that pushes some modern daredevils down, down, down into a mile-deep canyon on the end of a bungee cord.

It may be that some contemporary travelers would wish to retrace the footsteps of ancient heroes, and other intrepid souls might like to hold a séance in reverse, not summoning the spirits but going forth to meet them on their own ground. For everyone who fancies such adventure, here is a summary of the Homeric instructions for reaching the world below:

- At the outset, choose the one ghost you'd most like to see.
- Set course, then, for the north in a sizeable sailboat (note below all the items, from shovel to sheep, you'll need to take along), and let wind fill the sails until you arrive at a wooded shore on the edge of the ocean stream. Jump overboard in the shallows and, running through the surf, pull the boat onto the beach. You'll find an old cemetery in a grove nearby.

- There, keeping the ocean in sight, dig a deep, square hole, its sides measured by the distance between your elbow and your wrist. It is your gateway to the realms below.
- To unlock the gate, first pour three libations around the hole in this order: milk mixed with honey, sweet wine next, and water last. Then sprinkle white barley over the damp ground.
- By now the ghosts will be listening. Promise them that as soon as you return home, you'll sacrifice your best heifer calf. And promise the one ghost you have specially come to see that you'll also sacrifice a black lamb.
- Sacrifices must be made on the spot as well. You will, of course, have brought a ewe and a ram along on your sailboat, and both will have the requisite black fleece. When they have been slaughtered and skinned and their meat seared for burnt offerings, the hole will be brimful of ghosts.
- Take your sword from its scabbard to fend them off. The ghost you wish to see will soon appear to escort you downward.

At least, that's how Odysseus embarked on his tour. Interesting place to visit, but he didn't want to stay there. Homer doesn't say much, however, about how he got out, except that ghosts by the rustling, whispering, surging thousands finally pressed so insistently close that, caught by horror, he ran for his ship. And, yes, as all ninth-grade readers of the *Odyssey* know, he eventually made landfall on Ithaka, but not without more tribulations and skin-of-his-teeth escapes.

The ancient rumors about the Styx basin find two leading exponents in postclassical times. In the fourteenth century, Italy's Dante Alighieri promulgates them in the portion of his *Commedia* that treats of the Inferno. Three hundred fifty years later, John Milton's epic *Paradise Lost* gives them wide circulation in the English-speaking world. To some extent, both poets maintain the integrity of received wisdom. Dante bows to Homer and Virgil, those pioneer poet-geographers of the Styx river basin, but he nonetheless stations their ghosts near the front gate in a parklike area that is reserved for well-behaved heathens. It's clear, though, that Dante's tripartite afterworld, comprising Heaven, Hell, and Purgatory, owes much to his predecessors' division of the river basin into three jurisdictions. Dropping only the River Lethe, Dante also honors the Styx and its canonical tributaries. But in his update, the classical topography of Tartarus proper—lake, talus slope, swimming hole—is transformed by some hellishly dizzy geometry into nine circles, one of them pitted by ten *malebolge*, or dirty ditches. Dante, however, stays somewhat closer to tradition than does his British successor.

It must be granted, though, that Milton retains an evocative part of the time-honored geography and its nomenclature. In Book II of *Paradise Lost*, when Satan decides to sulk no longer but regain Heaven, some of his demonic minions break into song or sit on the sidelines twiddling their thumbs, while others "in squadrons and gross bands" start looking for a place less sulphurous and fiery in which to dwell. And their "flying march" gives them a fine aerial view of the rivers that drain the hellscape:

> *Abhorred Styx, the flood of deadly hate;*
> *Sad Acheron, of sorrow, black and deep;*
> *Cocytus, named of lamentation loud*
> *Heard on the rueful stream; fierce Phlegethon,*
> *Whose waves of torrent fire inflame with rage.*
> *Far off from these, a slow and silent stream,*
> *Lethe, the river of oblivion, rolls*
> *Her watery labyrinth. . . .*

But although Milton's geography is basically sound, his history is revisionist. Ignoring the accounts of earlier poets, dispossessing the deities hallowed by tradition, he places Satan on the throne and surrounds him with a "Stygian council" consisting of the Hebraic megademons Moloch, Belial, Mammon, and Beelzebub.

Though they both pluck part of their imagery from earlier reports of the Styx basin, Dante and Milton are clearly pursuing agendas of their own. Indeed, the reasons for writing about the place seem as many as the reasons for wanting to visit it. Homer's magical compositions, recited and sung to the music of a lyre, were staged as evening entertainments, which also served to recapture the nobility of a vanished past. Virgil, presenting an epic vision of Rome's princely beginnings, not only justified his patron's investment but also won approval from the emperor Augustus. Both Dante and Milton may certainly be viewed as moralists and Christian propagandists who employed their superlative poetic skills to promote particular theologies and sell the benefits of good behavior. But the sources of inspiration don't really matter. What counts is that the poems are, all of them, perfectly splendid.

The poems are also nothing but hearsay. I base this conclusion on a report that contradicts the one point on which the four poets and their contemporaries found agreement: that the Styx and its basin are situated below the surface of the earth. The report is written by a plainspoken eyewitness, my five-times-great-grandfather, who not only saw the Styx but surveyed it. Locating the river firmly in the world to which the living have everyday access, he also lists many of the plants and animals native to its basin. And his testimony about this wilderness receives corroboration from at least one later observer. Not long ago, I paid my own respects to the place and found it as I'd known it would be—breathtaking but partly tamed by the passage of 250 years and the clear-cutting, strip-mining, road-building, nearly resistless push of civilization.

I suppose, however, that the poets trafficking in hearsay should be forgiven. None of them had heard of West Virginia. To be fair, neither has the surveyor, for there is no such place in his day. In the 1700s, and indeed from its founding more than a century earlier, the Virginia colony stretched westward to the Mississippi. Not until 1863 will a breakaway fragment, antipathetic to the Confederate cause, be dubbed West Virginia and granted statehood by the Union.

His report in my hand, his image in my mind's eye, I watch the surveyor. He's Thomas Lewis, born in 1718 in County Donegal, Ireland,
and brought by his parents first to Pennsylvania, then to the part of Virginia where the Appalachian Mountains are rumpled up against the sky.
In 1744, he received his surveyor's license from the College of William
and Mary. Now it's Wednesday, September 10, 1746, and this dark-eyed,
dark-haired Scotch-Irishman, six feet tall with a sturdy, well-muscled
build, is plying his trade up here on the wooded crest of the Blue Ridge.
Despite the elevation and the season, it's a warm day. Sweating, he pushes his glasses back up to the bridge of his nose and readjusts the ear-
pieces. Though nearsightedness has kept him out of the military, it
hasn't stopped him in the least from conducting surveys.

Patience. It will take Thomas Lewis four weeks, six days, and many
adventures before he arrives at the River Styx.

On this survey, he aims to draw a straight and true line northwest
from the head spring of the Rappahannock River, on Bearfence Mountain in the Blue Ridge, to the head spring of the Potomac, on the Virginia
colony's side of Backbone Mountain, which also runs north into Mary-
land. The purpose of this exercise is to establish once and for all the
southwest boundary of the Northern Neck Proprietary, a long, narrow
tract comprising much untrammeled wilderness that sprawls westward
from Chesapeake Bay between the Rappahannock and the Pataomek, as
the name is spelled on some documents from the later 1600s, when
Charles II first awarded a patent for the land. But the patent holders and
the reigning monarch have disputed the boundaries ever since, never
mind that they've all been absentee landlords.

Now, however, Thomas Lewis has been commissioned to lead a survey on behalf of Thomas 6th Lord Fairfax (Milton, though willy-nilly ig-
norant of West Virginia, would have known the Fairfax name). Colonel
Peter Jefferson, father of a future president, represents the interests of his
majesty the king, who happens at this point to be George II. From the
survey's first day, the two companies, each comprising a survey crew and

support personnel including a farrier, have been encamped near the summit of Bearfence Mountain. They're raring to move forward, of course, but organizing for such a monumental job is slow business.

What I know, sitting in my easy chair and looking on, is that it has taken determination, fortitude, and a giant helping of optimism just to get started on a job that will have them messing around for weeks on end, rain or shine, through a never mapped (and certainly snaky) wilderness.

What Lord Fairfax's chief surveyor knows is that it won't be easy to run an arrow-straight boundary line for seventy-six miles through that kind of country. The survey companies will travel twice that distance, running a trial line on the journey out and firming up the true line on their return to the starting point. Thomas Lewis has known all along that he and the others will be wet, cold, hungry, bone-tired, and sometimes sick before the job is done. But he doesn't know yet, couldn't possibly have guessed, that he's bound for the River Styx.

Along the way, from the survey's first day to its last, Thomas Lewis records many details of the work. Using a quill pen, he jots them on the pages of his journal, a notebook $3\frac{1}{2}$ inches wide by $5\frac{5}{8}$ inches long, that slips easily into a pocket.

Though the survey was set in motion on September 10, the companies will not start working toward the headwaters of the Potomac for another two weeks. It is not, however, a period of inactivity. The first nine days are taken up by the work of assembling baggage horses and loading them with considerable gear (the survey's equipment is far more cumbersome than that of Odysseus on his excursion across the Styx, and its logistics far more complex). More critical is the task of fixing on precisely which of the myriad mountain rivulets is indeed the head spring of the Rappahannock. But while the teams labor, they also play. The two weeks are not without "a great Deal of pleasure & meriment" and "Some very good Syder." Nor are they without some impatience to get the show on the road; like children who don't want to wait but must, the surveyors fidget. Any distraction is welcome.

*Wensday 17th. Continued to pack
up our Bagage had our Instruments
try'd & notes taken of their Variations
or Different Directions. Spent the
Remaning part of the Evening in
our usual manner. This night
we were allarmed with a Quarrall
that happened in Capt Downs lane
amongst a Crowd of Drunken peple
the Rails & Staks of Capt Downs
fence Supply'd the want of Cudgels
which they apply'd with tolerable
good Sucses*

On Thursday, September 25, the head spring of the Rappahannock is
at last located. Or, more accurately, after several hard, steep days of to-
ing, fro-ing, and backtracking by the surveyors, Lord Fairfax's represen-
tatives and those of the king have reached agreement on precisely which
of the many small streams deserves that designation. And the survey
companies are off at last, scrambling over the summit of Bearfence
Mountain and heading down the western slope of the Blue Ridge. But despite high expectations, they're off to a dragging start, for the way down
the mountain is so difficult that the baggage train can't keep pace with
the surveyors, can't even keep them in sight. In the rapidly fading light
at day's end, the weary surveyors must climb back whence they came in
order to find their well-deserved dinners and their sleeping tents.

Thomas Lewis keeps track of the journey's progress and its events in
surveyor's fashion, pole after pole. Measured this way, in increments of
16½ feet, the 150-mile round-trip between the Rappahannock's headwaters and those of the Potomac turns into 48,000 poles, a distance that
somehow sounds vast enough to accommodate a flight to the moon—or
a descent to the River Styx.

... Thence N 43 1–2 W
180 pole 10 [feet] from River
764 po the first tope of the Peekd mt
920 another top of Dito
1000 x [crossed] a Br[anch]. Call'd the fountain of life
  from the Seasonable Relive it was to us
  the Day Being Exceding hot ye mountain
  very high & Steep we were allmost over
  -come & Ready to faint for want of
  Water

Pole after pole after pole, notching trees along the way to mark the survey's trial line, they drive northwest toward the source of the Potomac.

As I watch them ford countless streams and struggle over the densely wooded mountains, each successively more arduous than the one before, I am reminded of another, far earlier push across difficult and dangerous terrain: the Greek soldier Xenophon's march to the sea. He had brought ten thousand infantrymen to the service of Persia's Prince Cyrus, who coveted his brother's throne. After Cyrus's defeat, he led his contingent of mercenaries in retreat from Babylon across Asia Minor to the Black Sea. And as they marched, hoping against hope for a day of safe return to native soil, he made a record of events. And, like the journal of Thomas Lewis more than two thousand years later, Xenophon's record, the *Anabasis*, carries a refrain, repeated over and over, that almost metronomically ticks off progress toward the far-away sea and the voyage home: *enteuthen d' eporeuthesan*, "from that point they marched" so many stages and so many parasangs—so many days, that is, of twenty-mile marches and so many miles in addition to that conventional limit. Day after day, stage after stage after stage, Xenophon and his men press doggedly on until at last they do come safely to the edge of the sea and the final leg of their homeward journey. They shall see Greece again.

Thomas Lewis has also undertaken an anabasis, though not in

Xenophon's sense of the word as "retreat." Its primary meaning is "advance," and that's precisely what the survey companies are doing, day after day, pole after pole.

During the last week in September, asters and goldenrod bloom on the higher elevations. The leaves of the sourwoods, gums, chokecherries, and blueberries begin to catch fire. Gold, lavender and purple, red in a thousand shades from crimson to maroon, the landscape is newly decked out in autumnal raiment. And overhead, the hawks—red-tails, red-shoulders, broad-wings—ride the high pathways of the air on their southward migrations. With them soar both golden and bald eagles, also heading south. Though many days are still sweaty hot, the changing season brings more than its fair share of clouds and rain, and the nights turn chilly.

The advance of the survey is not smooth but proceeds in fits and starts. It's not simply that the weather becomes contrary, that much of the terrain is treacherous—steep, rocky, shin-breaking, and in places so well-nigh impassable that the horses must be led the long way around a mountain because they cannot be taken over its top. It's also that the people on whom the expedition must rely aren't always where they're supposed to be when they're needed. From the outset, the surveyors have intended to labor mightily for six days every week and devote the seventh to worship and rest, but when the provisioners fail to send fresh supplies in a timely fashion, the men cannot just stay put while the horses starve. Even on the Sabbath, it becomes "a work of Necessity . . . to press forward." And on the weekdays, the survey itself comes to a halt more than once so that its members may perform the more immediately vital task of hunting up food for animals and men.

Water isn't always at hand when it's needed either, despite the general abundance of springs, creeks, branches, and runs along the route. On October 7, a cloudy, rainy Tuesday, the surveyors ascend a mountain so steep that they take the horses over only with the utmost difficulty. By the time they make camp in the evening, the day's exertions have wrung them dry. But, as Thomas Lewis reports in his next journal entry, "We were very much put too for want of water we Could find no other than a Standing pudle wherein the Bears used to Wallow which we could not teast off till the last Extremity." I'm sure he did taste of it—water so full of mud and other particulates that it could have been chewed.

Hardships large and small do not, however, totally characterize the outgoing journey at this point. In the early weeks, the evening encampments are made sometimes at a homestead or a small settlement rather than on a wild stream bank or a mountainside. And Thomas Lewis is ever a man who appreciates "pleasure & meriment"—good company and good conversation, abundant food and potent drink. He does not hesitate to note such occasions, including one at which all who are present regale themselves with "Several Black Jacks of punch," a blackjack being a tankard made of tar-sealed leather. Nearsightedness notwithstanding, he also has an eye for the ladies, of whom there may not have been many in that sparsely settled land. After meeting a Mrs. Coburn some fifty miles into the journey, he takes out his quill pen to describe her with obvious delight as "a Bucksom lass."

On Tuesday, October 7, the day on which the surveyors are obliged to slake their thirst with bear-wallow potage, the Styx lies only one week in the future. The blaze of fall colors on the mountains is banked now, beginning to fade as the companies press diligently forward.

Wednesday, October 8: Notching a pine, an ash, two white oaks, and, last of all, two sycamores to mark the trial line, they cover a distance of 1,320 poles, or slightly more than four miles. Progress can't be faulted, but when the companies stop at a stream for the first truly fresh water in more than a day, somebody breaks the glass of the compass. Rain falls before evening.

Thursday, October 9: The sky is overcast, with more rain likely. Surveying instruments are laid aside for the time being so that the baggage animals can be moved a few miles up the line to the last settled outpost before the unrelieved wilderness closes in. This is the evening "Spent very meriley" in the company of Mr. Coburn and his buxom wife.

Friday, October 10: The survey companies remain encamped at the settlement, which lies on the South Branch of the Potomac and is destined to become the town of Petersburg, seat of Grant County, West Virginia. The daylit hours permit no idleness; everyone prepares as best he can for the plunge into the wilderness. Fresh provisions are packed in and made ready for the trek. The farrier, a man named Fumfire, sees to it that the horses are properly shod. The men have a chance at last to wash their shirts.

Saturday, October 11: Pole after pole after pole, the tally resumes. The men take up where they'd left off on the eighth, at the two sycamores. Up mountain and down and up again, moving at a straight, steady clip, they mark red oaks and white oaks, pines, a chestnut, and something that Thomas Lewis calls a "Cinamon tree," which might be (I'd like to think so) a sassafras, the roots of which may be boiled and steeped to make a spicy drink. At day's end, they have traveled another 2,880 poles. Nine miles! Camp for the night is set up on a creek bank. Here, not entirely worn out by the day's hard push, one of the men wounds a bear, which gets away.

Sunday, October 12: The Sabbath is honored at last by a respite from work. Several "Well Disposed hands" go hunting and kill one old bear and three cubs.

Monday, October 13: The day bristles with portents. Although it begins well enough with the routine ticking off of poles, progress comes to a near standstill just after the fourth mile. A prodigious number of deadfalls blocks the route, and the vines are so thickly interwoven that only with the utmost difficulty can passage be forced through for the men and the horses. But the companies chop and curse their way onward only to arrive at the face of a sheer, sixteen-foot cliff. The rest of the daylight hours are occupied by finding the least precipitous route to the mountain's necessary summit. When they at last struggle all the way up, they find that the summit is rocky but level and clear of timber, except for some gigantic maples and a few ash trees. There, fatigued and filthy, they make camp. It would seem a suitable place to spend the night, but something peculiar catches Thomas Lewis's attention. Peculiar indeed, or he wouldn't have taken the time and trouble to note the item even once, much less twice.

"Marshey," he writes, and repeats the word only a few lines later. It's as if the world has turned topsy-turvy, its low wetlands seeping upward to burst and spill their water across the sky. The ground up here on the top of Alleghany Mountain, the highest mountain Thomas Lewis has ever seen, is not merely level and rocky and largely clear of timber. It's a bog.

Marshy—the word has the ominous sound of a sibylline whisper. On this Monday evening, when he sees that the mountain is straddled by a marsh, is Thomas Lewis assaulted by premonitions? I'm sure that by now he foresees slow going in the days ahead and, pole after pole, new difficulties of an order more exhausting than anything the companies have experienced so far. And he can predict with hundred-percent certainty that there'll be no blackjacks of punch, no buxom lasses, no rest for weary bones until they all manage somehow to slog back out of this bruising wilderness and, like Xenophon's mercenaries, at last find the day of safe return. But camped on the weeping mountaintop, he cannot foresee that in fewer than twenty-four hours he'll reach the River Styx. Not only reach it, but cross it and know it for what it is.

Tuesday, October 14: One of the horses has wandered off. Most of the morning wastes away in a futile search. It's nearly noon when the survey companies shrug and take up where they left off the day before, on the strangely wet summit of Alleghany Mountain. After the first hundred poles, less than a third of a mile, they run smack-dab into a "Loral swamp."

Such places, also known as laurel brakes or laurel slicks, are vast rhododendron thickets that cover square miles of mountainside. Their roots find anchor in oozy sphagnum bogs, where the corpse-white moss soaks up water like a huge sponge. Their branches, "all most as Obstinate as if Composed of Iron," are so densely interlocked that daylight can hardly shine through.

There's no way around, at least not for surveyors who must run a straight, true line. Hacking their way through the iron branches, they struggle forward another three hundred poles. By one measurement, the day's progress amounts to little more than a mile. By another, the companies have leaped through time and space, for they make camp that night on the far side of the Styx. But let Thomas Lewis make his on-the-spot report.

> 406 poles × the River of Styx total for this Day
>   This River was calld Styx from the Dismal apper-
> ance of the place Being Sufficen to Strick terror in
> any human Creature ye Lorals Ivey & Spruce
> pine so Extremly thick in ye Swamp through
> which this River Runs that one Cannot have
> the Least prospect except they look upwards

Here he turns the page, dips his quill, and resumes writing.

> the Water of the River of Dark Brownish
> Cooler & its motion So Slow that it can hardly
> be Said to move its Depth about 4 feet the
> Bottom muddy and Banks high, which made
> it Extremly Difficult for us to pass the
> most of the horses when they attemp'd to asend
> the farthest Bank tumbling with their loads
> Back in the River. most of our Bagage that
> would have been Damaged by the water were
> Brought over on mens Shoulder Suchas

Powder, Bread and Bedclothes&c. We got all our
Bagage over as it Began to grow Dark So we
were Obliged to encamp on the Bank & in
Such a place where we Could not find a plain
Big enough for one Man to Lye on no fire
wood Except green or Roten Spruce pine no
place for our horses to feed And to prevent
their Eating of Loral tyd them all up
least they Should be poisoned.

In this true account, no avaricious ferryman brings his ramshackle
boat to the near bank. No hackling guard dog with three (or fifty) heads
flashes its long, yellow canines and growls in its many throats. But in a
darkness unrelieved by any fires, wolves are heard to speak, and leaves
rustle on chilly night winds with the dry insistence of ghosts.

The next morning, after a cramped, haunted sleep, the men stretch
themselves and stagger upright. Before they reach the end of the laurel
swamp, they must chop their way through an almost endless barricade of
iron branches. The footing is treacherous—deadfalls and rocks all overgrown with lush, slippery moss that also hides clefts and cavities. Avoiding one bad place often means stumbling into something worse. And the
horses, the hungry horses, get caught in the thickets, the rocks trap their
legs. Forward movement yields willy-nilly to the task of cutting branches and breaking rocks to free the animals. But after 630 poles, nearly two
arduous miles and as far as anyone will go this day, the laurel swamp is
left behind.

And there, before Thomas Lewis's very eyes, lies terrain as friendly
and welcoming as the Elysian Fields: "agood Spring timber'd land &
agood place for our horses to feed." Here they make camp and lie over
for a full day of rest and refreshment. Someone kills a deer, and on the
second evening there's venison for supper.

But this sweet place only imitates the Elysian Fields. Reaching it does not by any means signal an end to tribulations. The survey companies will reach the head spring of the Potomac in another week, on the evening of Wednesday, October 22. And they'll learn to their great satisfaction that the survey's trial line is almost on the mark. Running the true line back to the Rappahannock will call for only minor corrections.

But before they reach the Potomac, they'll face new troubles large and small. Colonel Jefferson's company sacrifices a day to a vain search for Fumfire, the farrier, who has strolled off down a trackless mountainside and gotten himself entirely lost. Or so it seems to the people who are looking for him high and low. In his wanderings, he bumps into the other company, which takes him along. But this kind of setback is merely an exasperating trifle in view of other circumstances that threaten lives. Some of the men suffer dizziness, faintness, and gripings of the gut. Provisions dwindle alarmingly, and everyone goes on extra-short rations to conserve the little on hand. There'll be no chance for fresh supplies until they get back to Mr. Coburn's. Fortunately, the skilled hunters among them are able to supplement the meager diet with deer and turkeys. It is not so easy to fill the huge bellies of the horses. At this point, the survey is pushed on as much by the need to find decent pasturage as by a long-ago commitment to do the job. But tight palisades of laurel keep barring the way. Thomas Lewis notes that he and the others begin to be afraid of entering the swamps. But they do because they must—and once in, there's no backing out.

After the Potomac's headwaters are reached, and his majesty George II's health drunk in spring water, the survey companies hightail it back to Alleghany Mountain. Though they're at work, running the survey's true line as they go, it takes them a mere four days to get there. Their appetites account for some of the haste, for the food supply is perilously low. But most of the hurry is caused by the hot and desperate desire to put thickets behind them forever.

On the mountain's marshy summit, Thomas Lewis pens a heartfelt sigh of relief: "Never was any poor Creaturs in Such a Condition as we were in nor Ever was aCriminal more glad By having made his Escape out of prison as we were to Get Rid of those Accursed Lorals." And the very next morning, they come all unaware on one of an upland bog's October virtues—cranberries. I can see the red juices staining their mouths and dripping down their beards.

Late on Tuesday, October 28—a long, hollow-bellied day of 1,900 poles—the companies arrive back at Mr. Coburn's. En route, one of Thomas Lewis's crew has surprised a "Statly Buck" and killed it with an ax. All other provender long gone, it is the only food his company brings into camp. But now they're home free; they've reached the Elysian Fields, the paradise gained only by crossing the Styx. Relief makes them down-right giddy. Over here, they engage in wrestling matches with some of the settlers. Over there, Fumfire the farrier is brought to trial for leaving the company to which he was assigned. He is sentenced to wear a bell around his neck for a week.

After this respite, Thomas Lewis, Colonel Peter Jefferson, and their men push through weather that is increasingly rainy and cold and suffer the usual delays in the delivery of fresh provisions. They finally make it back to the survey's starting point on Thursday, November 13. Here, at the head spring of the Rappahannock, they drink to Lord Fairfax's health and that of his majesty and fire off a nine-gun salute. And then they all go home to lead good long lives. My five-times-great-grandfather will not depart this world until 1790.

His 1746 survey endures to this day, marking private and public boundaries alike, separating farms, dividing county from county along its ruler-straight line. And his observations of the Styx and its basin have been corroborated by later visitors, notably Porte Crayon, or "Pencil Toter," as the artist-journalist David Hunter Strother styled himself. In an 1854 issue of *Harper's New Monthly Magazine*, Crayon published an illus-trated account of his adventures with a group of hunters in the Virginian Canaan, a mountain wilderness in what would, only nine years later, be-come West Virginia. It includes the present-day Canaan Valley, pronounced *kuh-NAN*, and also the Stygian route traversed by Thomas Lewis.

The landscape that greets Crayon and his companions is exactly the same moss-covered, boggy snarl of deadfalls, thickets, cliffs, and ravines that triggered fear in the survey parties of 1746. Reading words written a hundred years later, I am able to see more clearly through the ancestral eyes, for Crayon's descriptions and lively drawings add color and considerable body to Thomas Lewis's pared-down, somewhat laconic notes.

The fallen trees in the climax forest of the Styx basin lie alone or in huge logjam heaps. The giants among them measure as much as eighteen feet around and 150 feet in length. The moss-covered trunks look solid, but more than one member of Crayon's party has walked on them only to crash through up to the armpits. And the infamous laurel brakes, as Crayon calls the swamps, evoke the same dread in the hunters as in the survey teams. These primal thickets present a physical barrier so daunting that deer can find passage only through the thinnest places, and a bear must use much of its enormous strength to crash through. What's more, the hunting party's horses balk at entering a swamp—not only balk but flat-out refuse—unless a tidy passage has been cut for them by the axmen. Worse, it is rumored that men have lost their way in the iron tangles and wandered in circles until they died. The hunters are more fortunate, however, than their eighteenth-century predecessors, for they are not required to cut straight through but may choose, if they wish, to go around.

Good sense to the contrary, that's not always what they wish. On one of these occasions, the party's guides, cussing "like the army in Flanders," spend two hours clearing a path for the horses, which even then, tossing their heads and rolling their eyes till the whites show, must be persuaded to go forward. One of them promptly becomes so entangled that it takes an ax to cut him free. When everyone is well and truly swallowed up in the swamp, Crayon climbs to the top of a hemlock stump to watch the action and make a sketch or two. Later, he writes this account for *Harper's*:

*The footmen passed ahead of the horses and soon found themselves . . . up to
their knees in mud and water; they were throttled by the snake-like branches of
the laurel, and were frequently obliged to resort to their hunting knives to ex-
tricate a leg or an arm from its grasp. . . . The laurel waved up and down as
far as the eye could reach, like a green lake, with either shore walled by the
massive forest, and out of its bed rose singly, or in groups of three or four, the
tallest and most imposing of the fir species. The heads of our adventurers appeared and disappeared alternately as they struggled through; and whether
visible or invisible, the crackling of the branches, the rustling of leaves, and a
rolling fire of execrations marked their progress. All else was silent.*

The drawing that accompanies this description shows the laurel swamp
alive with a great confusion. Trying to free the horses, some men hack
away at the thicket; others, hollering loudly, slip on the slick mosses and
fall on rumps or bellies into the swamp. One man, his feet skidding out
from under him, finds his neck caught in the iron embrace of a laurel
branch.

The reason for pushing their way through the swamp—and the cause
of the execrations, struggles, and painful accidents—is that the hunters
are looking for a shortcut. A river awaits them, and they're eager to get
there. The swamp, however, pretty much takes the stuffing out of them,
and that evening they are too "worn and spiritless" to chase a passing
bear. But they force themselves onward. Finally they hear, "far below, the
rushing of the waterfalls."

The river, of course, is the Styx. Note that this report carries the first
historical mention of its cataract. But unlike Thomas Lewis, Porte Crayon does not know the river for what it is. He calls it the Blackwater, a
name that designates it to this day.

In the sweet benignity of early summer, I make my own journey to the
fabled river. In the winding lower reaches, wild yellow flags grow in
wide, random swaths along the banks. Cattails crowd the marshy edges.
Birds are everywhere: indigo buntings lisping from the tops of pines,

PASSING THE LAUREL.

common yellowthroats and chipping sparrows singing from half-con-cealed perches in the streamside underbrush, cliff swallows darting with calligraphic grace over the water. Islets of pinkish sandstone crop up midstream, most of them covered by a dense, green fur of shrubbery. The lower river is grey-brown, slow-moving, and reticent. It's lovely but much too contented with itself.

The upper river is another story. These days it's quite accessible by paved road and the immaculately maintained walking trails of Blackwa-ter Falls State Park. Hardened trails traverse the sphagnum bogs and part the infamous laurels that still rise thick on the mountainsides, their slen-der, supple branches locked together more tightly than any weave of hu-man design. A few purple flower clusters, afterthoughts of spring bloom, glow amid the glossy, dark-green leaves. Graveled paths and board-walks offer views of the river.

The Styx flows deep and sluggish in some stretches; in others, it slides nimbly around the rocks and breaks into shallow rapids. As truly report-ed by Thomas Lewis, the color is dark brown, almost black, stained by tannin from decaying leaves and bark. Along many sections, the rocky banks rise high and steep enough to daunt any horse struggling to climb out and gain a footing on dry land.

Hemlocks, oaks, and ferns grow out of the rocks, and young bass-wood trees with leaves the size of salad plates. A doe, browsing in the un-derstory, pays no attention to me and the other picture-taking people on a boardwalk only ten feet away. My film runs out, and I move on down the walk to a railed deck from which the falls may be observed.

Like any natural phenomenon, the falls of the Styx may be described in objective terms. A topographic survey quadrant at the ranger station tells me that the falls are located in the Monongahela National Forest at a latitude of approximately 39°06′30″ and a longitude of 79°28′70″. Their elevation is about 3,133 feet. A sign near the observation deck informs all and sundry that the cliff over which the river spills consists of the in-tricately fractured but resistant sandstones known to geologists as the

THE GREAT FALLS OF THE BLACKWATER.

Homestead and Conoquenessing formations, both of which yield oil, natural gas, and commercial brines. The cliff, sixty feet high and at least that wide, looks something like a cake composed of thick layers of rosy-beige rock. And the water pours down, down, just as Porte Crayon saw and drew it, except that his full cataract has been much reduced this year by summer drought. At the center of the cliff, one waterfall descends in a narrow stream but splashes outward when it hits an outcrop two-thirds of the way down. To the east, near the far bank, a larger waterfall comes down in a broad, silvery banner. And on the western bank, several slender ribbons of water flutter and glisten as they splash over the top of the rosy cliff.

But I'm also seeing something else, and seeing it with ancient eyes. Homer, singing across the millennia, would surely describe this river as "steep-running water," as he did the deep and whirling Xanthos that Achilles turned red with Trojan blood. Here indeed is steep-running water, vital and potent water that tumbles glittering down its canyon like braided light. Sounding water that plunges with a white and furious rush over its sheer cliff. Silent water that flows languid through its deep pools and becomes a black mirror reflecting leaves and clouds. Water that wholly possesses the world through which it runs.

How does Thomas Lewis know that this river is the Styx?

The question rises suddenly out of the black water. It leaps to the sunshot surface like a trout. And just as suddenly I know the answer.

It's necessary to retract my statement that all reports preceding that of Thomas Lewis are nothing but hearsay. Dante and Milton may still be ignored, for both poets, seeing no demonstrable reality in the earlier material, simply helped themselves to ancient details and used them quite selectively to lend color, shape, and resonance to their own visions of heaven and hell. But Homer and Virgil cannot be so easily dismissed. Their reports, I'm sure of it now, contain important elements of truth. Although it's most unlikely that these elder poets made their own visits to the Styx basin, both certainly selected their informants with great care,

choosing either those who had actually seen the place or, more probably, those who were trustworthy guardians of earlier eyewitness accounts.

My five-times-great-grandfather persuades me that Homer and Virgil
offer reliable evidence. First of all, Virgil gives him the physical clues by
which he can recognize the place. The surveyor of the Styx is, after all,
an educated man, beneficiary of a classical education—reading, writing,
arithmetic, and lots of Latin. (His eccentric spelling and arbitrary capi-
talization are hardly deficiencies but reflect the uncodifed practices of
the day.) Because the boy has been required, in the ordinary course of his
schooling, to read and parse the *Aeneid*, and very likely the *Odyssey*, it
happens that when the man comes all unsuspecting upon the River Styx,
he knows it instantly for what it is by Virgil's ancient description: On the
far side of a steep gorge, amid a measureless forest of pine and oak and
holly, through shadowy marshes, the cold, black river flows.

Then, just as Virgil's clues are accurate, so is the claim on his part, and
Homer's, that the only way to arrive at the blessed, bright Elysian
Fields—the only way to earn them—is to cross the Styx. Without toil
and pain, there is no true access to comfort and delight. The final element of truth in the old accounts is that it takes a hero to get there and
back again.

Of course, I do not see precisely the same Styx as that crossed by
Thomas Lewis, Aeneas, Odysseus, and the intrepid others. It seems to be
an intermittent stream, sometimes flowing in full spate, sometimes dry-
ing to a mere trickle, here disappearing underground, there pouring
forth in a great black flood. Rivers change their characters and courses,
mountains rise and wear away, earth shifts along its fault lines. No geo-
graphic features on (and under) earth are exempt from change.

And in just this way, reports made over the last few millennia about
any particular feature, such as the Styx, are also subject to the constant,
irresistible forces of erosion and accretion. Like geological formations,

speculations have piled up along with the hard facts, and both rest atop the bedrock of irrefutable truth.

Good evidence places one of the Styx's head springs in the underworld, and there's certainly another in the part of the upperworld now known as West Virginia. Why then should the Styx not find still another upwelling in the outerworld of space? And when tomorrow's explorers reach its astonishing banks, there shall be no lack of men and women, heroes all, to risk the dire crossing and return with new reports.

the

frog king

The place to find the frog king is in
the waters of a deep, dark well that lies beneath a tree in a great forest.
And when the golden ball you've been tossing blithely slips from your
fingers and falls down the well shaft, he'll rise to the surface. He'll try
then to make a bargain—your ball returned if you'll take him home. So
say the Brothers Grimm, who ought to know, though they issue a warn-

ing that such things have only occurred "in the olden days, when wishing still helped."

The forest that I walk through almost daily in the winter is more a
scraggly second-growth woods than a real forest, and I bring along
binoculars, not a golden ball. Nor is there a single well along the trail I
follow. But the good Brothers' warning may be ignored, for the winter
woods are so filled with enchantments that anything might happen, including the apparition of a frog that does not croak, does not say *ribbet* or
b'gump, but rather wheedles and cajoles.

The hope of being surprised by such a marvel is not, of course, what
brings me to the woods. The prime reason for taking a walk is Sally. In
the winter months, when rural freedom on our Carolina river is left behind for city living in the Shenandoah Valley, she cannot adequately
give her long Doberlegs any kind of stretch, much less a good one, in a
tiny, in-town backyard. We leave the Chief behind, for he much prefers
his indoor comforts, recliner and cable TV, to taking a chance on frost-
bite. He also stays home because the first and only time that he volun-
teered his services and actually took her for an outing, she met her first
and only (so far) skunk. Despite liberal applications of tomato juice and
baby shampoo, she wore a musky reek for close on half a year.

When Sal and I pile into the car and drive to the park, she is so eager
that her soft, uncropped ears perk all the way up and her whole body
quivers. This park, one of two owned by the city, is on the edge of town,
within its limits but surrounded by open farmland. When I stop in the
picnic-playground area atop a tree-clad hill and open the back door, excitement propels Sal through the air like a rocket. When she lands, she
streaks off down the trail. All I see for the next few seconds is a black-
and-rust blur moving nearly at the speed of light. When she returns from
this dash, the two of us move on at a more sedate pace. I can't begin to
guess what amazements will present themselves in the next hour plus.
But I do know I'll see something to wonder at.

But there's one thing I'm not likely to see, and that's a matter for won-der too. Where are the people in this park? It may be simply that winter's lowering skies and chilly winds keep them away. And when the snows come, the road leading to the top of the wooded hill is well-nigh im-passable without four-wheel drive—it's not on the city's agenda for plow-ing. Sal and I must wait for a thaw. Summertime may well bring a great passel of giggles and shouts to the playground; it may veil the picnic shelters in a day-in, day-out haze of charcoal smoke and the juicy aromas of grilling meat. But in winter, except for occasional people who hang out in the hilltop parking lot on milder days to fiddle with their cars or listen to their boom boxes, the place is well-nigh deserted. The trail al-most always belongs to Sally and me and nobody else. Good thing, for not everyone understands that a Doberman stretching her legs is not launched on a vicious charge.

Winding unobtrusively through the woods just below the hill's crest, the trail makes a grand circle. We start at the trail's beginning—it does have other access points—and walk the wrong way around. Wrong way around? Yes, for numbered stations, one through twenty, mark the route. When a federal grant two decades ago enabled the town to develop this wild addition to the park—the tame part, with tennis courts and pool, surrounds a nineteenth-century manor house at the property's other end—the Recreation Department opted not only for slides, swings, and picnic shelters but also for a trail that would attract walkers, runners, and fitness buffs. Each station along the way bore a brown-on-white sign with written and pictorial instructions on just what to do in that partic-ular spot—swing your arms this way or bend your torso that. In addition to the signs, some stations were variously equipped with chinning bars, rings to swing from, a beam to balance on.

Station six, built beside a cluster of red and white oaks on the hill's western side, was evidently designed for frogs. Positioned a yard apart and placed in a slow curve, six posts the size of railroad ties lie on the ground. The sign's pictograph shows a human figure executing what looks like a bunny hop onto and between the posts. But the legend clearly reads":

Frog jump

over hurdles.

I say "each station *bore*" and "some *were* equipped." That was in the early days. When I began these rounds ten years ago with Sal, then a bouncing pup, the trail was neatly trimmed and the stations well marked. She shows a touch of hoarfrost on her muzzle now, I'm considerably more creaky than once upon a time, and many of the stations have fallen into desuetude. The signs at thirteen, eleven, and ten have toppled into the underbrush; the balance beam at nine has completely disappeared. Honeysuckle tangles and the canes of brambles—winter-brown blackberries, silvery raspberries, red dewberries covered with a fine, dense fur of prickers—close in on the path and reach across it. After a high wind or a hard snow, deadwood clutters the way—branches always, and sometimes a whole tree. So it's not just winter but a decade of neglect that keeps almost everybody else away and lets me happily imagine that the trail belongs only to Sal and me.

It was laid out in a clockwise fashion, but we go widdershins. There's reason, of course, for such contrariness. The trail is rarely flat but mounts and descends, up, down, up again, as it circles the hill. The section between stations nineteen and twenty is the most precipitous of all, a slope that looks nearly vertical to me but is more likely a steep thirty degrees. I'd rather skid and slither down to the bottom than huff and puff up to the top.

And around we go, Sal and I, around and around, November through February. She dashes forward on the trail, pauses to sniff, hares into the woods, returns to check on me, and dashes off again. The dry leaves crackle as she passes. Do I exercise according to the posted instructions? No. I do not frog jump, push up, bend, or swing; neither do I chin. I amble and often stop, sometimes sitting on the benchlike wooden structure at station eleven or leaning on the upright posts at station eight. And I wait, watching, listening, wondering what sort of gift will present itself this time. And these things happen:

A bird soft and grey as a snow-bearing cloud flies swiftly past at the level of my chest. The flight makes no noise at all. Screech owl.

Sal runs ahead and startles something that crashes through the underbrush in my direction. White-tailed doe.

On a mild November morning after a night of rain, I spy several mushrooms lifting large caps above the trail-side grass. They're fresh and plump, nor does the pressure of my finger bruise the pores. The species is not only edible but absolutely choice. Boletus, destined for a lunchtime omelet.

With a great flap-flap-flap of wings, a large bird lifts off from its roost—and a second bird, a third, a fourth. Necks stretched out, they look like geese, but geese don't perch in trees or take to the air with such commotions. Wild turkey hens.

After a hard freeze, the earth crunching beneath my boots, I notice something that looks like a red tennis ball lying on the trail. And there's another, along with a small yellow something. In the olden days, an orchard must have stood near station eight. Apples gone wild, and pears.

I come to the grassy, tree-shaded meadow, not much bigger than a queen-sized blanket, that lies off the trail between stations eleven and ten. Sal's leaping upward, trying to catch the large, brown animal she's put up a tree. Wheezing, grunting, it scrabbles higher and higher still. Its sharp rodent teeth could cause her grievous injury, but the creature's completely intent on upward escape. I'm flabbergasted. I thought this animal was earthbound. Groundhog.

During a bright blue January thaw, warm enough to make me shed my jacket, a sweetly plaintive song rises at station thirteen and again in the near vicinity of stations four and three. The tune is not at all familiar, and I cannot imagine what bird this is to be singing in winter when sensible birds do nothing but chip and buzz and squawk. Oh. Frogs.

When we're home again and I tell the Chief about frog-song in January and speculate that wood frogs might be giving voice, he's no help at all. "What I'd like to know," he says, thinking of bullfrogs, "is how they get themselves up on those lily pads when they weigh so much."

But that question has no bearing so far as the trail is concerned. Just as there is no well here to furnish the frog king with a watery domain, there's not one lily pad to be his throne, and certainly no pond in which water lilies might grow. Nor have I discovered any stream or spring. From station twenty to station one, the trail seems bereft of water. Sal attests to the lack by slaking a great thirst the instant we get home. The only drink she's ever found along the trail has come in the infrequent form of snow. Once home, even on the snowy days, she hightails it to her water bowl and drains it dry. And if we do not refill the bowl quickly enough, she heads for that bottomless fountain, the commode. But there must be water somewhere in the trail's vicinity. How else to account for frog-song? How else to fulfill the general requirement of all frogs, wood frogs included, for water in which to spawn?

It's frog-song, of course, that puts me in mind of the frog king. And in these modern democratic times, when wishing supposedly gets you nowhere, he might make do with something other than a well. But what might appeal to his royal fancy? A parking lot puddle? Rainwater in the bottom of a picnic-shelter trash barrel? Amid the trail's other enchantments, surely there's a place for the frog king. And if not the king himself, then a frog prince would do.

He might be in disguise. Occasionally, Sal and I do encounter other talking creatures. We come across their sign on every walk—sometimes the imprints of an unfamiliar paw or boot, and always the cigarette filters, candy and gum wrappers, plastic cups, soda cans, and bottles for beer and strong drink. Once, a fairly new pair of men's underpants was abandoned at trailside near station nineteen. Recently, the steep incline between stations twelve and eleven was strewn with miniature marshmallows. But it's only on one round out of every twenty that we actually meet human beings, though we do not catch sight of the same faces year after year. People appear once or twice or, less often, for a single season before they vanish, never to be seen again. When we do meet them, it's usually one at a time or in groups of two or three, but once the unexpected apparition of a Doberman immobilized a mittened and mufflered gaggle of ladies out for a winter bird walk. I made some introductions, Sal wagged her nubby tail, and we parted amicably.

Bumping into Bird-Watchers might have been predicted. So might our regular meetings, early on, with the sweat-suited Exerciser, who jogged clockwise around the trail and obeyed the commands on all twenty signs. And we were surely bound to meet the Young Man with Big Dog in those early days when the trail was trimmed and tidy and all the signs erect. I never learned the young man's name, but the dog was Wags, a large, bouncy, mostly white collie mix. He and Sal would play for a vigorous minute before she and I went on our widdershins way. But most of the other people have been wild cards—and surprised as could be at meeting us.

Take the Trailkeeper. For several weeks, I'd noticed his work, the berry canes and vines cut back, the overhanging branches neatly lopped off. We first met him as he came striding down the hill toward station eight with his woolen watch cap pulled low almost over his eyes. He stopped short at seeing us. Sal didn't seem to bother him a bit. It was I who made him need to account for himself. "Peaceful place. Nobody here. Keep things neat," he said, showing me a pair of pruning shears before he scooted off, quick and shy as a deer. We saw him five or six times more. That was four years ago. No sign of his services now remains.

And there were the Equestriennes, three strapping big girls on strapping big horses from one of the farms at park's edge. I'd known about them for a month—horse apples on the trail and great raw gouges where heavy hooves had skidded downhill and destroyed the turf. But they hadn't known about us—not till Sal met them one morning. She's a quiet animal but summoned me then with peremptory barks. The girl in the vanguard began railing about leash laws and how I'd broken them. The local ordinance stipulates only that a dog be under control, either on lead or by command, but it's not easy to interrupt a strapping big diatribe. Sal came when she was called, of course, and sat till the procession lumbered by. White letters on square, mocha-brown signs now announce "NO HORSEBACK RIDING."

But the Mountain Bikers did no damage. Their occasional spoor appeared on the trail several months before we met them. After a rain, muddy patches were sometimes imprinted with the tread marks of narrow tires. Once, the tires cleaved a fresh six-inch snow that was otherwise marked only with the tracks of juncos, field mice, cottontails, and deer. On our single encounter, they almost literally ran into Sally as they rolled trailward down the steep access path near station seven. When I rounded the corner, she was wagging her tail at the bikers, a man and his not quite adolescent son, who had stopped stock-still. Both gazed at us through wire-rimmed glasses; in keeping with current fashion, both were clad in helmets, windbreakers, and biking shoes of throbbing pink, electric yellow, neon green, and Day-Glo magenta. We stared at one another. Then the man said sternly, "We have never before seen anybody—not anybody—on this trail." And off they sped clockwise as Sal and I continued our walk the wrong way 'round.

In Sally's fourth winter, on those days that we took our walk during the noon hour, another twosome would frequently show up—the Cheaters. That designation may not be fair, but why else would a man and a woman, in their old thirties or young forties, choose to spend a lunch-hour break in a parking lot at the top of a cold, windy hill? That kind of behavior is often accounted for by hanky-panky. In every weather, fair or freezing, he arrived in his car and she in hers. Most often she'd slip over to his front seat and sit close to talk and cuddle. Cuddling may have been a necessary measure for keeping warm; he never kept his engine running, not even on the most frigid days. But once, when a bright, mild day gave its blessing to a February lunch break, Sal and I came across them leaning on the balance beam, at that time still in place at station nine. They quickly pulled apart their hands. I said hello and proclaimed Sal's gentle nature. "Evenin'," he said, in the country fashion that reckons any time after high noon to be on the verge of dusk. We did not see the two of them again, not on the trail nor in the parking lot.

This year, it's we who have been startled, not the Hunter with whom we'd been sharing the trail all unaware. At first, I dubbed him the Lurker, for he is given to hiding behind one tree or another near the trail's beginning. There he stands so motionless against a trunk that he might well be part of it, a large burl or a broken branch. The first time we saw him, he tore loose, lurched upright, and whistle-whispered through his dentures, "You seen any game?" Game? Turns out he's a good old boy who drives a pickup truck about as faded, dented, and rusted as he is. Coming to the park right often to do with aging eyes what he used to could do with a shotgun, he still-hunts here for whatever shows itself, always the big grey squirrels, sometimes the little red ones, now and then a deer, we ever seen one of them? After we got acquainted, he's cough or shuffle his feet to let me know where he'd taken a stand. Then we'd greet each other and trade brief reports on recent sightings of game. And I have a glimmer of just how fortunate I am: Anyone who lurks in this small-town park is infinitely more likely to be a Hunter than a Mugger. But I haven't seen him since just before Christmas, when six inches of snow wrapped the park in a winter blanket.

Strange creatures along the trail, oh yes, and who's to say what may or may not materialize? It's in this tenth season of trail walking, around the time that we first meet the Hunter, that Sally discovers the spot in which the frog king might be camping out.

As I stand at station three trying to spot the pileated woodpecker that's cackling like a maniac, she races back to me from somewhere up ahead. Water glistens in her whiskers. Several fat drops decorate her nose. Her chin is not just wet but sopping. She's dived headfirst into a drinking bowl. What luck! But what around here holds water? And where? A guess puts its location somewhere off-trail in the open, leaf-carpeted stand of oaks and hickories between stations three and one. After station one, there's a steep ascent to the parking lot.

On the next walk, Sal remembers where she found refreshing drink, but she doesn't show me. The time after that, though, I catch her in the act. The place is right at trailside, a short hop and jump past station two. From shoulders to rump, she is visible, but her head is thrust between two slender tree trunks. And the sound of her lapping is loud and fluent.

Water! Sunlit water, sky-reflecting water, a great bowl of water held in a tree!

The tree is a pignut hickory—or a set of quintuplet hickories, with not just two trunks but five, all grown so closely together at the base, wood locked into wood, that they are inseparable. Then, a foot from the ground, they divide, each leaning slightly outward and rising thirty feet into the air. That quinquepartite base holds a good gallon of rain or melted snow. It freezes, of course, when the temperatures plunge, but in such weather any sensible frog, royal or not, will have settled into hibernation. And Sal can wait until we're home to drink her fill.

As for the frog king, he hasn't importuned me. Not yet. But who's to affirm or deny the disappearance of the days when wishing still helped? And even in this newer day of general skepticism and outright disbelief, there's nothing outmoded in making a wish—on a star, on a birthday candle, or for the hope that the act of wishing represents. Someone wise in the ways of water—and far senior to the Brothers Grimm—knows something that may not have occurred to them. He's Herakleitos, who speaks from the far bank of the fifth century B.C. but is famous to this day for remarking that, because water flows, no one can step in the same river twice. And Herakleitos has also said, "The presence of gods in the world goes unnoticed by people who do not believe in gods."

Thank you very much, I'll keep on wishing.

and this way the water comes down at the gorge

We gave Charlie to the Bullpasture, his chosen river, on a bright blue, ten-degree day three weeks before Christmas.

Not one cloud floated on the sky, and the distant sun lent a shine without warmth to wet stones and the rushing, braided flow. As always, the waters leaped loud and vigorous down their mountain-guarded channel. And on the surface of that fluent white noise, other smaller sounds bobbed like dry leaves—the slow, deliberate scolding of black-capped chickadees; the high, thin whistles of golden-crowned kinglets. It seemed that the hemlocks on the steep river bank, and the Virginia pines, had been decked with living ornaments. Feathers fluffed out, the little birds hovered and hopped, searching the branches with talkative but ceaseless industry for the fuel, the seeds and dormant insects, needed abundantly to keep their tiny engines spinning hot in such cold weather. A shivering day, but it was filled with clear, clean light. And the occasion held a sense of fitness, a flush of joy, that could not have been predicted when we'd planned the expedition from town to the mountains and the rolling river.

We'd come here in solemnity and merriment because my mother stubbed her toe. But that's a tale for later on. First, I'd like you to see the Bullpasture and how it comes down at its steep-sided gorge.

Showering and springing,
    Flying and flinging,
Writhing and wringing,
Eddying and whisking,
Spouting and frisking,
Turning and twisting,
    Around and around
With endless rebound!

"Yiii-yi-yi-yi! Eeeee! Yeee-*hah*!"

Shrieking, shouting, yelling their fool heads off, young'uns mob the summertime river. Male and female, early teens, a merry horde of at least two dozen has disembarked from the old blue-painted bus, labeled Spottswood Baptist Church, that's parked up on County Route 678. Surely they raced pell-mell down the rough logging road that clings to the side of Jack Mountain, the road that I've just descended slowly so as not to jostle aging knees. And surely they cast off their clothing without one second of delay; heaped like jetsam from a spring flood, jeans and T-shirts litter the riverbank. Now, clad in bathing suits and bursting youth, they clamber over rocks and boulders, slide screaming down the sloping, three-foot waterfall on their rumps, splash the length of the deep and leisurely swimming hole, and climb out to start all over again. Several girls, commanding inner tubes on the backwater calms of the swimming hole, paddle themselves round and round like oversized whirligig beetles. With grace and the utmost nonchalance, one boy shoots that algae-slick waterfall standing up, arms extended for balance, as if he were riding a skateboard or, better yet, surfing. The girls cheer. And the fully clothed man standing on my rock notices me and lifts his eyebrows.

Rock? That's somehow too small a word. This wide ledge of ancient grey dolomite veined with a subtle dusty pink juts more than a third of the way across the river. Another ledge equally large thrusts toward it from the opposite bank. Between them they channel the river's flow into a narrow opening through which it spills down the low, slippery falls where the young'uns are shrieking and sliding. A limestone boulder big as a good-sized shed rests squarely in the middle of the opening, almost dividing the falls in two. One of the boys has clambered atop it, king of the castle.

I smile. "What fun! What fabulous fun!"

The man smiles too. "Yeah, good place for the young folks on a hot summer day."

"And the not so young. Always has been, always will be."

"You come here often?"

"Every time I can get unplugged from the old routine. How about you and this ecstatic mob? Looks like they've found paradise right here on earth."

"Reckon they have. I been carrying the Youth Group from church out here, oh, maybe a dozen years now. And you know, this is the first time there's ever anybody else come down to the swimming hole whilst we were here." He averts his gaze, looks down at my lichen-encrusted rock, and shifts his weight gently from left foot to right. He seems uneasy.

I natter away at him: Long bus ride from Spottswood, yes, but got to be well worth the time, and how splendid, how absolutely fitting to a handsome summer day, to see people having such huge fun in a wild and usually lonesome mountain river. Rocks and falls and long, slow swimming hole, the one small piece of ground that's level and clear enough for pitching a tent, the fireplace built of river stones, the fragrance of ferns and damp earth, the calls of birds, the little rustlings of who knows what—people just can't help abandoning themselves to the pleasures of the place, and that's as it should be, long as people don't also abandon their trash when they head for home. And I tell the Youth Group's shepherd about the fisherman disturbed by me and my long-gone English springer one April morning about a week after trout season had started. He scowled at intruding woman and dog. He turned his back when I said, "G'mornin'." When dog approached wagging her tail, he gathered his tackle and empty creel and stomped off, cracking deadfall sticks beneath his heavy tread. And, mounting a motorcycle stashed out of sight, varoom, varoom, he roared up the logging road. As if there weren't room, and to spare, for all three of us, plus a nice mess of rainbow trout.

The young'uns are still shouting and splashing and showing off. The man is still uneasy. "Always pick up our trash, we do. Leave the place cleaner'n when we found it. Um—I don't know."

"Don't know what?"

And he comes out with it. "Who owns this place? The state or somebody? I mean, do you know if it's all right to be here?"

For the first time in more than a decade of bringing teenagers to the swimming hole and its natural water slide, he's encountered a stranger. It's not that he feels he ought not to be here. It's that he's been caught. *Forgive us our trespasses as we forgive those who trespass against us.* The man needs reassurance.

"River belongs to everybody," I tell him. "Public waters."

"This public land? Those signs up top, alongside the road?"

Those signs, printed on tough, weatherproof Tyvek plastic and nailed to tree trunks, are posted by Virginia's Game and Inland Fisheries Commission. They read:

TROUT FISHING WATERS
special license needed for trout in
addition to regular fishing license

Below this legend, an arrow pointing upstream or down or in both directions at once indicates the waters affected by the double-licensing regulation.

That's all the information that the signs contain, but they give a lot of people odd ideas—that the state owns the entire riverbank or that only duly licensed fishermen are allowed to put themselves beside or in the water. Or, in a sadly common misinterpretation, that no one at all is supposed to be down here: The mere existence of the signs is read as a warning that the land itself is posted, NO TRESPASSING, KEEP OUT! Truth is, the state does own considerable acreage along this wild bank of the Bullpasture, much of it bought with money from hunting and fishing license fees and managed now for wildlife and forestry. The federal government owns much of the far bank and Bullpasture Mountain rising above it—a sizeable tract that's part of the George Washington National Forest. And anyone who wants to, who doesn't shoot deer out of season or cut down timber to which he's not entitled, can pretty well go traipsing at will through National Forest or the commonwealth's Wildlife Management Area. In these domains, the risk comes not from people but from timber rattlers and black bears. But it's not always possible to tell public from private lands, not unless the property is posted, or occupied by somebody's cabin, or barred at its entrance by a padlocked gate.

I explain about the signs put up by Game and Inland Fisheries, that they're not meant to keep anyone away. As for this access to the river, the land with the old logging road traversing the side of Jack Mountain at a steep slant, it's mine.

"Yours! We're much obliged." The man who stands on my rock smiles, then frowns. He turns toward the hooting, hollering, splashing river and starts to lift an arm.

"No, no. Stay."

"Day's getting on, and I reckon we been here long enough."

Is his pleasure somehow spoiled because, with no warning at all, ownership has assumed particularity? It wears my face, my grey hair. It may as well wear my name. I tell him who I am and hold out my hand.

He shakes it briskly and quickly, sends a piercing whistle to the kids, and beckons them ashore. They groan but respond promptly. It's plain that they like and respect this man who has brought them to the river's cooling rush. As they gather their clothes and towel themselves from sopping wet into a state of bus-worthy dampness, I try to remove the shadow from his day, to assure him that such bright and innocent enjoyment is his for the taking next month, next year, the year after.

"Young'uns need rivers the way gardens need rain. Come anytime, come back when you want. Just get in your bus and arrive."

"Ma'am, I do thank you kindly." He's stiff and formal.

"You're welcome here, I mean it. Otherwise, there'd be a gate up top, and some nasty signs."

He nods politely and starts to walk away. I've not assuaged his feeling of trespass. But before he leaves my rock, he stops stock-still. "Lord a mercy!"

He'll be back, he and his flock in their blue-painted bus. Here, in a stony crevice, in a minuscule pocket of soil, a wild rose has taken root, lifted itself toward the light, and unfolded one small, pink blossom. Here in the gorge, the rocks themselves burst into flower.

And thumping and plumping and bumping and jumping,
And dashing and flashing and splashing and clashing . . . .

It's not just young'uns come splashing and dashing down through this water. So do fish, notably trout. Inland Fisheries stocks the Bullpasture with rainbows and brookies, many of them raised in the hatchery at Coursey Springs over in the next valley, that of the Cowpasture River. But some of the fish that flash and jump here never saw artificial pools and aerators and human attendants of any hatchery. The river still holds fish that were born to its flow, wild fish.

"Native species, oh yes." It's Nevin Davis talking, retired postmaster of the tiny crossroads community that's located just past the downriver end of the gorge at the point that the Bullpasture joins the Cowpasture. "Last year, young man name of Stone was down by the junction fishing, and he saw something strange in the water, something very large swimming and jumping. And he mentioned it to Bobby Lockridge, who was standing on the bank. Bobby got him a stick, waded right into the river, and started using that stick as a club. What he brought out was a brown trout every bit of thirty inches long."

That story would have tickled Charlie, a wilder man than Bobby Lockridge ever thought of being.

It runs through the reeds,
*   And away it proceeds. . . .*

Near the end of the gorge, springwater runs glistening through watercress and bulrushes down to the river. It trickles over and under the wall of river stones that somebody long ago placed around the spring to create a pool from which the clear, ice-cold water can easily be dipped. Ready access to this spring probably accounts for the location of Charlie's cabin. From source to cook-pots and washbasin, it's not an unmerciful chore to tote full buckets a mere hundred feet.

Charlie didn't exactly build the cabin. He christened it though, most likely with good bourbon, and called it Spit 'n Whittle after two male pastimes of long and honorable standing. In my ten-year-old perceptions of Charlie and his ways, this name was irrevocably connected to Squat 'n Giggle, a term that he used occasionally in speaking of some activities reserved strictly for women. But my mother, his sister, often called the cabin The House That Jack Built, not because it was the tumbledown trigger for a series of disasters—it wasn't, not in the slightest—but because a man named Jack Marshall had sold Charlie the land and helped him rebuild an existing log structure that had reached a state of true dilapidation. The two of them took apart that old dwelling. They cleaned stout logs that had been cut in the nineteenth century, set them back in place, and chinked the cracks so well that neither wind nor rain could find its way inside. They did not try to save the original fireplace and chimney but built them anew with smooth-worn river stones. Bullpasture Mountain's oak trees gave them shakes for the roof; and its chestnuts, the split rails for the fence with which they enclosed the clearing in which the cabin stands. When it was done, the old-new cabin contained three rooms—living room, bedroom, and kitchen—and a screened porch that stretched across the full length of its upriver end. This was a porch for eating supper, for rocking and reading away the rainy days, for snuggling on a cot to watch fireflies and fall asleep to the river's soft and incessant rush.

And these things occurred when Charlie was in his twenties, before the big chestnuts on Bullpasture Mountain were wiped out by blight, before World War II swept him up, a captain in the National Guard, and sent him to Omaha Beach, from which he returned home alive but crazy, full of shrapnel and nightmares.

But in those years that he was gone for a soldier, years that also put my father in an army uniform and dispatched him to the European theater, cabin and clearing and cool-welling spring did not languish but were put in the keeping of women and children. My mother had gone back to her mother for the war's duration. Whenever she could save, beg, or borrow enough gas-rationing coupons for the fifty-mile trip from town to the Bullpasture gorge, she packed us all up—my two brothers and me, our

MOUNTAIN CABIN - "SPIT & WHITTLE - WILLIAMSVILLE, VA.

grandmother and her dog Mona, a liver-and-white English springer spaniel—and gave us transport to The House That Jack Built. One of my brothers was a toddler then, and therefore useless; the other, only two years younger than I, had his virtues, though on the trip he needed a brown paper bag to vomit in, especially when our mother navigated twisting, precipitous mountain roads. Despite such fraternal inconveniences, I was doubly transported, not only carried to the river but carried away on a flood-surge of excitement: Young'uns need rivers as gardens need rain.

The fun began as soon as we arrived at the rough dirt road giving access to the cabin. That road was a washed-out, deeply rutted, axle-breaking affair that Charlie had dubbed Featherbed Lane. At its top, Joe and I, the two elder children, were allowed to get out of the car and stand on its running boards for the short, bumpy ride down to the cabin.

From that instant of arrival till our return to town, we played. I didn't see it then as play—and as a temporary, adult-engineered shrugging off of war. For me, everything we did was simply part and parcel of everyday life. And if we did things we didn't do in town, such as spitting in the yard when we brushed our teeth, well, we were just following the river's dictates. Even Mona Springer followed them; she knew by the prickling of her canine instincts that she'd been born and bred for water, and she went for a vigorous swim every chance she had.

Joe and I played variously or together at all the games the Bullpasture had to offer. We went wading, we turned over rocks to catch crayfish, we pole-fished, we climbed atop the limestone boulder as big as a shed and zipped down the algae-slick waterfall and loafed through the calm reaches of the swimming hole. And for extra excitement, we left bathing suits on the boulder and skinny-dipped. The spring, where we watched water striders and ate peppery watercress, was my second-favorite place. The place I liked best was the big rock ledge opposite the one I now own. Its surface bore curious lichens of palest peach and grey and green. Feathery ferns curled upward out of its soil-filled crevices, along with grasses and even some saplings. Ants, beetles, and spiders lived among them, and swallowtail butterflies flitted overhead. Below the waterline, snails crawled wearing black conical shells, and minnows darted. I named the big rock Mother Nature.

What games our little brother played I do not know. To a staggering, puling baby such as he, Joe and I couldn't have paid much mind—he was hardly human. Mona Springer was far more fun. Hindsight, tutored by my own years of motherhood, tells me that he was fully occupied by tagging along with our mother as she entertained herself by traveling back to the nineteenth century and taking on the role of a self-reliant country woman. Indeed, at that time and in that remote mountain hollow, we might well have been in the nineteenth century, for war had largely deprived us of automobiles, and the cabin had never been fitted out with amenities taken for granted in town—electric lights, water from a tap, an indoor toilet. A one-hole outhouse served us, except for my grandmother, who was exempted from its use because she had her very own throne handy in the bedroom. Actually, it was a wooden armchair with a hole cut into the seat and a chamber pot concealed below. I didn't mind going to the outhouse by day, when snakes and spiders could be seen and avoided, but after dark it lay at the far end of a fearsome journey—despite the framed Scotch-Irish prayer on the living room wall that sought the good Lord's deliverance from ghoulies and ghosties and long-legged beasties and things that go bump in the night. We did use candles and flashlights, though, to help the good Lord keep darkness at bay. I think hot meals were prepared on a woodstove—they must have been, though cooking was never my business in those days, nor was it an activity in which my mother or my grandmother ever participated when we came to the cabin. The reason that we kept our distance from the kitchen was part of my grandmother's game, not my mother's.

Providing water, fetching food and ice—those were my mother's responsibilities. On a shoulder yoke, she carried buckets of sweet, clean water two at a time from the spring to the kitchen. Sometimes she also brought back a fresh-picked handful of watercress to add a cool, faintly spicy tang to the suppertime tossed salad. For the grocery expeditions, she loaded our small brother into a wheelbarrow and, with Mona Springer keeping them company, trundled him up Featherbed Lane, across the iron suspension bridge that spanned the Bullpasture below the mill dam, and around the corner to one of the two general stores that the crossroads community supported back then, along with the mill, the post office, a service station, and a sturdy red-brick Presbyterian church. And back they would come—woman, child, dog, and wheelbarrow— with bread, brown eggs from local chickens, milk and butter from local cows, as well as other staples—peanut butter, jelly, hotdogs—needed by growing children. That was how my mother played it—close to earth.

But my grandmother's game was regal, a game for a lady or, better yet, a queen. Full-brimmed sunbonnet tied under her chin, corncob pipe she did not smoke clenched in her teeth, her disguise was that of an old-timey mountain woman. But I look back and think of Marie Antoinette playing at dairymaid or shepherdess. Every morning, supporting her weight on a rustic walking cane, she moved with a slow and heavy majesty to the porch. There she ensconced herself in a rocking chair to issue commands and hold court. Her minions leaped to do her bidding, to raise or lower the awnings according to the sun's position, to bring her books or tea or sewing basket, to make polite conversation. We were not, however, allowed to mention the four unspeakable S's—Sin, Sex, Sickness, and Servants. The Four Horsemen of the Apocalypse would have been more welcome. For me, it was easy to avoid the first three topics; I didn't know much about them anyhow. The fourth was quite another matter, for her minions at Spit 'n Whittle consisted not only of daughter and grandchildren and a handful of local ladies who walked down Featherbed Lane to come calling and pay their respects but also a servant, Ella.

Desert or jungle or sparsely populated mountain hollow—if there were a servant to be found, my grandmother would find and employ her. Born to Southern gentility, brought up with little money but with a thoroughly Victorian understanding of a lady's role, my grandmother never soiled her clever hands with dust, dirty dishes, laundry, or infants. Nor on Ella's Sundays off did she cook but arranged that we all be taken two miles up the road to Mrs. Jack Marshall's white frame gingerbread house and well-laden country table, where we dined invariably on roast chicken, mashed potatoes, and green beans. My grandmother did not, however, opt out of domestic affairs, no indeed, but figured instead as a force to be constantly reckoned with: Her task was to make sure that everything was done that needed doing, from cleaning to cooking, and with the proper tools, ingredients, and good manners. Oh, she was fierce for good manners, and among the proprieties that small fry were to observe was staying out of Ella's way. As a result, I hardly remember Ella, except as a hefty black presence who reigned in the kitchen, slept in the shed, and saw snakes everywhere.

There were snakes to be seen all right, good ones like blacksnakes, scary ones like timber rattlers, though surely not so many as Ella reported with shrieks and trembling. But on the better-safe-than-sorry principle, my mother carried a snake stick for defense whenever she fetched springwater or escorted children on the trail past the spring to my big Mother Nature rock. She may never have used this stout five-foot pole, may never have even spotted anything on which to use it, for the habit of most snakes, benign or venomous, is generally to avoid confrontation. I certainly saw no snakes anywhere by the Bullpasture. And that wasn't fair, because my brother Joe did see one—"big, beautiful!"—a copperhead.

In 1943, at the tender age of ten, I was sent into exile. Adult authority bought the specified clothing, sewed on name tapes, and packed me off for two months at a girls' summer camp in West Virginia: You can learn to ride, dear, and canoe and play tennis, you'll be with youngsters your own age. That was the summer Mona Springer went for a swim and drowned, pushed over the milldam by a strong current as my mother and Joe looked on with helpless eyes. In 1944, I served a second term at camp. That was the summer of Charlie's return home. In 1945, my father came back from the war and moved his family up north, unreachably far from the silent water welling and sparkling in the cold, clear spring and the tumultuous water tumbling and rushing down at the Bullpasture's five-mile-long gorge.

> *Smiting and fighting,*
> *A sight to delight in;*
> *Confounding, astounding,*
> *Dizzying and deafening the ear with its sound.*
> *Dividing and gliding and sliding,*
> *And falling and brawling and sprawling,*
> *And driving . . . .*

A river of cattle surges down the dirt road. Some are solid red, some red and white, and still others roan. All of them wear large, sharp-pointed horns. The herd's animals, more than a hundred strong, low and bawl and roll their eyes. Onward they plod, and dust rises from their hooves in billowing clouds. Several men on horseback accompany the herd. Riding at the sides or in the rear, they keep it in line and chivvy it onward with whips or sturdy sticks. But no mounted cowboy sets the herd's pace. That task is performed by a footman, a portly, dignified Negro who wears the clothing typical of any prosperous Shenandoah Valley farmer—hat with low crown and wide brim, dark suit-coat cut nearly to his knees, white shirt, and neatly knotted cravat. In his hands, he holds the sturdy lead ropes that are tied to the flaring horns of the two steers right behind him. He walks, they follow, pulling the rest of the herd in their wake. They've crossed through Panther Gap down at Goshen. Another day, and the drive from the valley to summer pasture in the mountains will be over. The return to a lowland farm won't take place for many a month, not till November or December brings a hard, black frost.

And that's how it was in the spring of 1853, when Porte Crayon (as

the artist David Hunter Strother chose to call himself) picked up his pencil, toted it to the scene, and made a finely detailed black-and-white
drawing of "The Drove" en route from winter quarters in the valley to the
high, grassy, floodplain meadows of the Cowpasture and the Bullpasture.
To his lively illustration, it's fair to add color, for printed sources from the
1800s almost invariably describe the valley's stocky, scrubby, no-breed
common cattle in shades and mottlings of red, red, red. As for the dust
and the noise, well, throughout the nineteenth century, the Wild West
was no farther away than western Virginia. Nor did roaring, ripsnorting
cattle drives confine themselves to such legendary routes as the
Chisholm Trail. Men on horseback and men on foot drove the valley's
herds not only westward to the montane pastures but north and east to
market in cities such as Philadelphia and Baltimore. Both kinds of drives
got under way when valley farmers started raising cattle in the mid-
1700s, a century before Porte Crayon picked up his eponymous pencil.

1853: Despite the year (and despite the opinion of Porte Crayon, who
held the prejudices of his time), it's probable that the Negro footman at
the head of the whole bellowing parade was a free man, for the valley
never cottoned much to holding slaves. The herd may even have belonged to him. But whoever their owner, these cows and steers were being moved off the farm up into the mountains to save the tender summer
crops. In those days, cattle were wild, free-ranging animals. The fences
they encountered were never meant to keep them in but rather to keep
them out—out of the house yard, out of the kitchen garden, out of the
corn. And if a farmer and his neighbors hoped to raise and reap decent
crops, they made sure first off that their cattle were sent into exile at
summer camp.

The drives from the lowlands over Panther and Buffalo gaps and up
into the lush mountain valleys continued, though on a less exuberant
scale, through the first two decades of the twentieth century. One of
Charlie's two elder sisters, not my close-to-earth mother but the other
one, the dreamy, hedonistic sister, recalled accompanying their Uncle

THE DROVES.

Willie as he took his cows from the farm down on Middle River for summer grazing up in Highland County near Monterey. That drive occurred in the days of the First World War. And cattle are still being driven in the vicinity of Monterey, though the phenomenon is much reduced in distance and size, with only a small herd of beef cattle mooing and shuffling along a country road for a few miles as a local man takes his animals from one of his farms to another nearby. In a burst of nostalgia, the weekly paper makes proud report of this quite parochial but richly noisy and colorful event.

Bullpasture, Cowpasture, and yes, Calfpasture: Each flows through its own valley to make a trio as magically complete as any congeries of three, from the three bears to the Trinity. The springtime cattle drives afford one explanation for the placing of such names on the land. Beginning with calves and ending with bulls, it holds that the three river valleys, with their excellent grazing, were named for the order in which the animals tired on the long trek to the highlands.

Charlie once kept a cow. That was in postwar days, after he'd taken a wife and sold Spit 'n Whittle. Twiddles was the name he gave his cow because it described what he did to her udder in order to milk her.

But it likely wasn't cattle at all that figured in the naming of the three rivers and their three valleys.

> *From its fountains*
> *In the mountains,*
> *In its rills and its gills,——*
> *Through moss and through brake*
> *It runs and it creeps*
> *For a while till it sleeps*
> *In its own little lake.*

The Bullpasture wells ice-cold out of ancient rock up there close to the crest of Jack Mountain, which rises near the West Virginia border.

Down the steep mountainside it trickles, slowly at first but with increasing strength and speed as it gathers in water from countless tributary
springs and brooks. It races and tumbles down to its wide floodplain, and
there, with Jack Mountain on the east and Bullpasture Mountain on the
west, their long, lean ridges looming dark for miles against the sky, it begins to dawdle. Now winding this way, now wandering that, it takes its
own clear, sweet time to meander the twenty miles down to the gorge.
And the valley through which it loafs is a lush green lake of grass, as bare
of other vegetation as a prairie. Sheep drift in small, white, woolly clouds
across its treeless surface; cattle graze, cattle in every color of the bovine
rainbow, from black through brown and red and beige to creamy white
and every patchwork possible therefrom. This valley, like its two coun-
terparts, is pasture indeed. It has provided pasturage for centuries, perhaps millennia.

Imagine autumn. Imagine fire. Not only are the mountainsides ablaze
with maple leaves gone gold and scarlet, but real flames lick yellow, orange, red at the stiff frost-killed meadow grasses. Purposely kindled,
fanned by a rising wind, the many little fires grow and join forces, spitting, crackling, burning the valley floor from end to end. Clouds of
smoke roll grey and pungent, high as the mountaintops, into the air. In
spring, new shoots will poke up fresh and green through the blackened
earth. And the herds of bison, animals that shun the woodlands, will return to graze and grow fat. It is Indians—Shawnee, Cherokee,
Delaware—who put the dry grass to the torch each year, as soon as hunting season ends, so that the river valley stays clear of trees and thus continues to invite annual pasturage by these most excellent providers of
meat, hides, sinews, and bone, these great shaggy sources of individual
human life and the life of the nation.

By 1800, the bison were gone from western Virginia. Fifty years before that, white settlers had begun bringing their red cattle into the
mountain valleys. The English names that were placed on the valleys in
the 1700s did not speak, however, of scrubby domestic livestock but

rather of the larger bovine mammal, noble and primeval as an aurochs, that had grazed time out of mind in river-sweetened meadows. Calfpasture, Cowpasture, and Bullpasture: The lush green valleys were named first, and their names later slipped onto the rivers. The Cowpasture River was first known in English as Clover Creek, and the Bullpasture, also reduced in name to the half-pint status of a creek, was called Newfoundland.

But species identification of the bull, the cow, and the calf may not be so easy after all. Just the other day, someone threw out the suggestion that these designations could have referred to elk, an animal that ranged the high valleys in abundance and endured the human pressures on its populations three decades longer than the bison did.

Elk? Domestic cattle? The eastern bison? Charlie, a willing victim of unbridled imagination, would have rejected all three possibilities. I can hear him now: "All this limestone, all this shale, used to be a ocean right here where the Bull and the Cow and the Calf come down. Use your good sense. They was whales."

> *Through meadow and glade,*
> *In sun and in shade, . . .*
> *Here it comes sparkling,*
> *And there it lies darkling. . . .*

I remember waiting for Charlie to accomplish the daring feat and win his bet. I fully expected to lose, no question about it. If he said he'd do something, he meant it. And if he said he'd swing from the crystal chandelier in my grandmother's dining room, then that was a promise as good as gospel.

The war raged on in Europe, but Charlie's wounds had brought him back to the States. The army sent him to the newly constructed Woodrow Wilson military hospital, so named because its one-story wooden barracks stood row after drab brown row only a few miles east

of the town that was the birthplace of the country's twenty-eight president. The town was also Charlie's birthplace and, in my view, the more
illustrious because of that little-known fact. When he was strong
enough, the hospital gave him leave on weekends. He'd come to town,
to the red-brick Victorian house he grew up in, for Sunday dinner with
his mother, sister, nephews, and niece. He'd sit opposite my grandmother at the old, highly polished walnut table and dine on roast chick-
en, rice, tomatoes stewed with sugar and bread, homemade biscuits and
lemon meringue pie or, if we were lucky, devil's food cake of a heavenly
richness (every bite prepared, of course, by Sadie, the cook, who was Ella's urban counterpart). Sundays, I glutted myself on good food and
Charlie's presence.

Let other girls worship the celluloid likes of Cary Grant, Gary Coop-
er, and Clark Gable. Charlie was real. From gleaming captain's bars to the
glitter in his eye, my hero was real. His real and toothy smile stretched
almost from ear to ear. His real and gallant mustache scratched my
cheek when he gave me an avuncular kiss. Best of all, he treated eleven-
year-old me as if I, too, were real and not just a child. How the matter of
the chandelier-as-trapeze came up, I do not know (I think I dared him).
But he took me on, accepting the idea as if it were perfectly ordinary. Not
only that, but he gave earnest of his good faith by taking a ten-dollar bill
from his wallet and putting it in escrow with my mother. How, then,
could I *not* believe him? (And how could I pay him when I lost?) I adored
the man.

Joe remembers quite another event. Charlie kept a bottle of bourbon
hidden in the pantry underneath the paper bags my grandmother saved.
Joe knew of the stash. Somehow evading vigilant adults, he and a nine-
year-old contemporary marked the liquor line, emptied the bottle, re-
filled it to the mark with cider vinegar, and tucked it back beneath the
bags. Later, a hearty, drinking man's gulp straight from the bottle. A
choking sputter. A howl of sheer, knowing outrage. By some domestic
miracle, Joe went unpunished.

I waited Sunday after Sunday, but the chandelier remained untouched. The ten-dollar bill eventually migrated to my pocket. Charlie had set me up.

And grumbling and rumbling and tumbling,
And clattering and battering and shattering. . . .

Terror swept down at the gorge the summer I was twenty.

By then, Charlie was an insurance salesman living with wife, Twiddles the cow, and sundry goats on a tiny farm close to town. And he was drinking more whisky than wallet or body could easily afford. He no longer owned the cabin and its clearing, along with the spring and the big Mother Nature rock, but they hadn't entirely slipped out of the family. My father had bought the place. Not only that, but he, my mother, my brothers, and my two postwar sisters had bade farewell to the big-city north and moved themselves happily south to the small and gentle town of my mother's growing up. College and something more—a stretching of wings, a flight from the nest—kept me on the far side of the Mason-Dixon line. But in the freedom of early summer, I'd brought a school friend to stay at Spit 'n Whittle for a week so she could see for herself that all my talk about the Bullpasture was not hyperbole but, at best, an inadequate approximation of the cool, wet, ever-rushing truth. In the early afternoon of a placid, blue and gold June day, we'd put on bathing suits and sneakers, grabbed snake sticks, and gone for a river walk. But walking was soon traded in for soaking up sun. Just upstream of the water slide between the Mother Nature rock and the corresponding rock on the opposite bank, half a dozen limestone boulders, rising three and four feet out of the water, had been flung mid-river long ago, like a great grey set of giant's blocks. We each chose a boulder, climbed aboard, and stretched out. With sun pounding down and stored heat rising from the stone, lying there was a hot and soporific business.

Of the three rivers, all are cradled in mountain valleys, all meander shallow and lazy across the wide meadows, all contain rippling, trembling reflections of heaven, but only the Bullpasture thrusts down a gorge as it looks for the sea. Five miles above its junction with the Cowpasture, the mountains on either side of its leisurely floodplain slam almost shut. From that point till it reaches its sister river, the Bullpasture is locked by steep, forested cliffs into a channel nearly as constricted as the waist of an hourglass. Shadows linger here long in the morning and make their return early in the afternoon, for sheer mountain walls permit the entry of full sunlight only in the fleeting hours on either side of noon. But in their seasons, with nowhere else to go, the raw, dark chill of winter and summer's most stifling heat hunker down on the gorge and settle in. Always that steep-sided canyon prisons the river as it carries its fluent burden. And sometimes there's more water than the space available can easily handle. When the spring rains that often last for days come pouring down, or the brief but torrential summer thundershowers, water may saturate the soil of the Bullpasture's upper valley. The river rises, it overflows its pebbled bed, and the wide meadows drown beneath a sprawling flood. Obeying gravity's irresistible pull, the flood rolls downhill and enters the rock-bound narrows of the gorge.

Terror was barely audible at first. It began as a distant yet steady rumble superimposed on the river's incessant rush. In no time at all, that unplaceable sound grew larger, louder, closer.

There wasn't time then for fear. There wasn't time even to think. We first saw the water as it rounded a bend two hundred yards upstream—a wall five feet high, turbid, frothing, all a-roar. It bristled with deadwood. It hurtled at us with runaway force. Then it crashed over us, careless and swift.

I don't know how we had the wit to grab our snake sticks before the wall struck, nor how we hung on to them as we were torn loose and tossed downstream. But wedged between stones on the riverbed, the sticks became upright posts to which we clung. We were safe then. And the riverbank was only twenty feet away. The muddy brown water ran high and strong, debris churned around us, but one step at a time, with the help of those sticks, my friend and I could reach solid earth. Or she could, and did. I couldn't. Not able to feel the stick in my hands, I stood there shuddering and completely numb. The moment we stood on the riverbed, the moment I knew we wouldn't die, shock hit like the flood surge after a hurricane. Again and again, the ghost of a spaniel was caught in the current, whirled down the millpond, pulled over the dam. But terror receded. The body sensibly insisted on dry clothes and a stable footing. Without difficulty, I made it back to firm ground.

The odd part was that there'd been no indication, none at all, that terror would sweep down the summer river. The skies had been cloudlessly blue. No distant thunder had warned of heavy rains upstream. Indeed, no rain at all had fallen within the week. Whence had that moving rampart come? It appeared out of nowhere like water released by the lifting of a floodgate or a sudden break in a dam. I conjecture, decades later, that its source was some breached impoundment upstream, a far pond perhaps, or one created by beavers. It is not conjecture, however, but plain fact that my first-ever intimation of mortality came down at the gorge.

> . . . *in this rapid race*
> *On which it is bent,*
> *It reaches the place*
> *Of its steep descent.*

"He was a quiet little boy," my mother says of her brother Charlie. "Serious and self-contained. Always very well-behaved."

"A real straight arrow—that's the picture I have," says Joe. "He was an Eagle Scout for one thing. Then he graduated from VMI."

She nods. "But he never really wanted to be a soldier. He would have attended the University of Virginia, gone into the law, but there was no money. He went to the school that offered a full scholarship. It was the war put him back in uniform."

"War, yeah, the lottery character of war—a bullet has your name on it or it doesn't, and you begin not to care. I remember when Charlie came home," Joe says. "He wasn't a bit quiet then, and everything out of his mouth was goofy and funny, *insane* funny."

> . . . *gleaming and steaming and streaming and beaming,*
> *And rushing and flushing and brushing and gushing,*
> *And flapping and rapping and clapping and slapping,*
> *And curling and whirling and purling and twirling . . . .*

In the spring of 1944, three months before Charlie drew a losing ticket in the D-day lottery, I encountered a poem by a man in love with the sounds of water. The venue was the seventh-grade English class taught by Miss Huntley. Encountered? No, that verb is far too hesitant. I leaped in, starting at the summit, and slid with great glee right down a rhyming, chiming waterfall of words. And the words lack any meaning whatsoever except in their music and the way that they start in short lines at the top of the page and spread out, increasing in length and uproar, as they plunge down and down and at last find rest in the pool of silence at poem's end.

I didn't know then what I know now, that the poem (if indeed it deserves that honorable name) is a bad one, not art but artifice. It speaks not at all to the human condition but presents instead a facile exercise in rhyme and rhythm and onomatopoeia. It imitates the cascade for which it's named—"The Cataract at Lodore," which descends to Lake Derwentwater in England's Lake District. The man from whose pen this imitation rushed and gushed was Robert Southey (1774–1843), one of the Lake Poets, along with Coleridge and Wordsworth, and indisputably the least of the three.

Even so, somewhat wiser now than in the seventh grade, I still find slick, quick, shoot-the-chute thrills in Southey's glancing, dancing, sounding, bounding, straying, playing, toiling and boiling cataract of

words. There's reason, of course, that pleasure in such a peculiar con-
struct continues to this day. Eyes discover little resemblance between
Southey's water and mine. Lodore's precipitous cataract comes down in
a fashion quite unlike that of the Bullpasture, which never tumbles from
any great height but slips through its gorge over a slow, irregular series
of stair-step falls. For years, the highest falls on the Bullpasture, and the
only one over three feet in height, was the milldam at the gorge's lower
end. But where eyes fail, ears recognize a likeness. From the moment I
first leaped into Southey's stream of sound, it became memento, talis-
man, magical chant. It spoke my river's language in my river's voice. I
could take it with me everywhere, to school, to summer camp, to the
postwar north, and everywhere I could listen at will to water's insistent,
ceaseless rush; everywhere feel its purl and tumble in my own veins.

> *Rising and leaping,*
> *Sinking and creeping,*
> *Swelling and sweeping . . . .*

And changing, yet staying the same.

In 1972, the iron suspension bridge that linked the eastern, Featherbed Lane side of the river with the crossroads village on the western
bank was replaced with a concrete model. A year or two after that, a
spring flood took out the dam and the millrace, which hadn't been used
or mended for years. Where the dam once stood, spanning the Bullpasture from mountainside to mountainside and stemming its flow into a
deep, almost lightless pond, nothing is left but a crumbling trace of concrete footing. Unimpeded now, the river runs shallow. The mill itself, last
in a succession of mills occupying the site since the late 1700s, had been
closed decades before, in 1941. When it was operating, though, in the
days before power lines had been strung across the mountains and
through the rural valleys, the mill did double duty, grinding corn by day
and making electricity for everybody in the vicinity after five o'clock.

Nowadays, only the millwheel remains, sitting across the street from the post office like a monumental piece of rust-patined geometric sculpture. The mill was dismantled. Its pieces, carefully numbered for reconstruction elsewhere, were taken to a town twenty-five miles up the Bullpasture Valley and piled neatly beside the firehouse. And there, someone of incendiary bent burned up the whole shebang.

The crossroads village has done almost as good a job of disappearing as the mill, though Nevin Davis, the retired postmaster, whose house shares a party wall with his former place of work, states that two things have increased to the point of being 'just ridiculous": the traffic zipping through and the trash left behind in its here-and-gone wake. All else of human works and enterprise has suffered diminution. The population, which stood at forty in 1969, has shrunk to no more than a jot and tittle of that number, and some residents are that in name only, for they live not nearby but on outlying farms just a shade closer to the crossroads than to any other hamlet. The general stores were closed long ago; outside one of them, the rusted gas pumps lean like old tombstones. Weekdays, only the post office, with doors still open for business, seems to hold the designation "village" in place. On Sundays, as they've done since 1859 and cattle-driving days, minister and congregation at the redbrick Presbyterian church perform that task.

Though he lived into the mid-70s, Charlie saw little of these changes. The need to earn a living not only took him away from his farm and its animals but removed him from the Shenandoah Valley altogether. He and his wife packed up and relocated themselves in urban circumstances near Washington, D.C., a right far piece from the mountains and the Bullpasture. When he came back for occasional visits to his native ground, I didn't see him, didn't even know that he'd checked in, for my own grown-up life kept me in New England or the Midwest. And when not drink but a slow cancer killed him, his death took place east of the mountains on alien soil. It was several years later, toward the end of the

'70s, that Charlie finally came home. His widow gave his neatly packaged ashes to my mother, who stored them in a closet and forgot they
were there. Nor did she remember them until, at the end of the '80s, she
moved from a very large house to more manageable quarters.

Flux is the order of the day, the year, the millennium, and always has
been. Yet, by nature or circumstance, some things seem more resistant
than others to change. One of these is Spit 'n Whittle. Its access and environs aren't quite the same as in Charlie's day; Featherbed Lane has been
mended to smoothness, and the woods have been allowed to encroach
beyond the now-sagging split-rail fence so that the clearing has been reduced by half. Pileated woodpeckers play in the shadows. But as the
twentieth century races pell-mell toward the twenty-first, the cabin built
with nineteenth-century logs stands foursquare and sturdy. The present
owners, a group of men from the traffic- and people-congested flatlands
around Washington, D.C., call it the Beaver Falls Hunting Club. (Have
they ever heard of Featherbed Lane or Spit 'n Whittle? And how about
Squat 'n Giggle?) The club members have closed in the screened porch
where my grandmother used to hold court and turned it into a bunk
room; they've tacked a new porch onto one end of the cabin and made a
roofed walkway between the kitchen and the woodshed where Ella used
to sleep. These are minor, practical alterations; they hardly count. In November, after stalking white-tailed deer from dawn to dusk, the hunters
warm themselves at a fire that crackles and glows on the river-stone
hearth set in by Charlie. And the branch water in their bourbon comes
from the spring at which my mother used to fill her yoke-borne pails.
That spring, though cleared of watercress, still wells up sweet and icy-
cold and is still contained by the low limestone wall in a clear pool on
which the water striders dart. The overflow still trickles glistening
through ferns and bulrushes to the river. A path still follows the riverbank
from the spring to the big lichen-covered rock and the water slide falls—
Beaver Falls, as the club calls it, though that's a name bestowed in recent

years. Beaver are far more likely to be found in the Bullpasture's lazy, easily dammed upriver reaches than in its rapid tumble down the gorge.

If anything's been granted immunity to change, it's the river. Though
the structures built by people rise and fall, and people themselves live,
work, and die, the river has endured, pure and constant, an unspoiled
gift, a natural truth. Or so it has seemed until now. There's talk that a kind
of farm new to the pastures will soon move in; poultry growers in the
Shenandoah Valley are looking to expand their operations. New laws,
however, expressly forbid expansion in the counties that now support
the annual hatching and raising of half a million Thanksgiving dinners
and an even greater number of fryers, roasters, and broilers for Holly
Farms, Perdue, and the take-out buckets of KFC. Why clip the poultry
growers' wings? Because large flocks of chickens and turkeys produce
their weight in droppings, and the leachate from droppings quickly pol-
lutes groundwater and streams. Such legislation-after-the-fact closes the
chicken-coop door after the fox has grabbed and gone. That sly raider
hasn't entered the pastures counties yet, but apprised of its coming, one
local government has put in place a new land-use ordinance. But it does
not limit the number of poultry houses on one site, it does not call for
water sampling, nor does it provide for enforcement. It is, alas, as tooth-
less as a turkey. And, with nowhere else to go nearby, the poultrymen
will break their bounds and sweep in like a rushing spring flood.

For now, though, the river runs constant and true. The water comes
down at the gorge, its clean white noise as necessary and calming and
close to silence as a steady pulse. It is still the same changeable yet
changeless water that comforted my youth, and Joe's. Listen to him for a
moment. (The round-faced eight-year-old, who traveled clutching a
brown paper bag, has become a tall, grizzled, contemplative man, a poet
and an artist, the modern-day counterpart of Porte Crayon.)

He says this: spring morning—
        the Bullpasture River

shivers off the mist   below the waterfall
                                        swirls of upbound mist
                                        brighten the young leaves
This: the Bullpasture River
    murmurs down the rocks—
    a rainbow's shadow   sunrise
                                you shake out the sheets
                                by the bright river
This: with each lightning flash
    the loud river
    gorges more of the land   after the storm
                                   turgid waters fall—
                                   a mockingbird cries
And this: coddling
                        the moon
                        the river

True, all of it. Charlie would have drunk to that.

And so never ending, but always descending,
Sounds and motions for ever and ever are blending,
All at once and all o'er, with a mighty uproar;. . . .

"When shall we go to the river?" my mother asked not long before Thanksgiving.

I said, "After the holidays, after life settles down. Cold in those mountains this time of year. January maybe, if we get a nice day."

"Sooner. Before Christmas. Ashes in my closet, you see—they're just *not* convenient." Her tone was peremptory. She pointed to her left foot and told me that her toes were bruised because, when she'd gone that morning to select clothes from the small and unfamiliar bedroom closet in the small and manageable dwelling she'd leased, her toes had suddenly, unexpectedly banged into Charlie. Awaiting who knows what occasion, he had been stored for a good dozen years in the dark recesses of the master-bedroom closet in the house my mother had recently sold. That closet, of a size capacious enough to match the grand dimensions of the house, had easily held clothes on hangers, shoes on racks, and luggage at the back, with an ample corner left over for Charlie, who took up no more space and was no more noticeable than a shoe box.

"I cannot bury him as I did your father," she said. "This house is *rented*."

Twenty years earlier, she'd put my father's ashes beneath a fifty-foot Norway maple that he had planted as a sapling in the backyard of the house just sold. A bronze plaque with his name and dates marks the site. Maple tree and grave had been conveyed, of course, to the new owner, along with the rest of the property. But when one of us suggested that she take along the plaque and a good square of earth when she moved, she did not pause to consider such a notion. Our father was quite happy, she averred, beneath his tree in his own backyard, listening as he had in life to the freight trains passing half a mile away, though there were certainly fewer trains these days than there used to be. And for herself, she expected, please, an equally suitable resting place, one that had given her much pleasure during her life. Or she'd come back to haunt us.

Long acquaintance with an earthly place and great delight therein—those were her criteria. We had no choice. We could take Charlie nowhere but to his river in the gorge between Bullpasture and Jack Mountains. When the day chosen dawned frigid but bright, Joe drove us out from town.

And it was he who carried Charlie down the logging road. We'd opened the package in the car and left its outermost wrapping there, a small cardboard carton still bearing the metered stamp of United Parcel Service. The carton had held a sturdy box of dark-brown molded plastic that in turn contained a transparent, heavy-duty plastic bag closed with a twist-tie and filled with light grey, almost silvery powder. Brown box in one hand, Joe used the other to steady our mother, fragile and cautious with the weight of eighty years. With slow ceremony, we made our way down and down, the river sounding its processional uproar, the kinglets and chickadees singing a descant.

She stood on the riverbank watching as Joe and I walked out on my rock. There, near the waterfall, we linked arms and gave Charlie to his river. The ashes swirled, spreading out in a milky cloud. We gazed at them until they disappeared. Afterwards, incredulous but smiling, saying yes, oh yes, we talked about the day, how joy had astonished us.

Bullpasture pours down into its sister stream. Cowpasture descends into the James, the James into Chesapeake Bay and thence to the ever-surging pastures of the sea.

And this way the water comes down at the gorge.